P9-EKC-993

1492

The Year of the New World

Piero Ventura

1492

The Year of the New World

G. P. Putnam's Sons   New York

Giovanna Spadini collaborated on the text.
Andrea Ventura collaborated on the maps.

Published in 1992 by G. P. Putnam's Sons,
a division of The Putnam & Grosset Book Group,
200 Madison Avenue, New York, NY 10016.
Originally published in 1991 by Arnoldo
Mondadori Editore S.p.A., Milano.
Published simultaneously in Canada
Printed in Spain
Book design by Jean Weiss

Library of Congress Cataloging-in-Publication Data
Ventura, Piero.
[1492. English]
1492: the year of the New World / Piero Ventura.—1st
American ed. _ p. _ cm. _ Includes index.
Summary: An account of Columbus's voyage links descriptions of
life in various countries in fifteenth-century Europe with those of life
among various Indians in the New World.
1. Fifteenth century. 2. Columbus, Christopher. 3. America —
Discovery and exploration—Spanish. 4. Indians—First contact with
Western civilization. 5. Renaissance. [1. Renaissance.
2. Columbus, Christopher. 3. Indians. 4. America—Discovery and
exploration—Spanish. 5. World history.] I. Title.
CB367.V4613 1992 909'.4—dc20 91-26217 CIP AC
ISBN 0-399-22332-0
Artes Gráficas Toledo S.A.
D.L.TO:1814-1991

10 9 8 7 6 5 4 3 2 1

First American Edition

Contents

The Old World

What was happening in 1492, and how did people live then? Of course there was no radio or television, movies or newspapers. The printing press had recently been invented, most books were still written by hand, and it took about a month for news to spread from one end of Europe to the other. And yet pilgrims journeyed thousands of miles to visit Rome and other great Christian sanctuaries. Despite the hazards of pirates and highwaymen, and the inconvenience of customs duties, traders took their merchandise far and wide. Scholars went from one university to another and felt at home wherever they went, because a common language, Latin, was spoken. Great artists moved from court to court to add luster to rich and powerful ruling families, both old and new. Soldiers of fortune fought for whoever offered them the most pay. Princes and rulers inspected their realms, sought new alliances, and took great interest in conquering new lands. People traveled a lot, for many different reasons, and those who knew how to write often kept a record of what they saw.

We can take an imaginary journey through the Europe of 1492 as seen and experienced by imaginary persons of the time. Then we will follow Christopher Columbus's actual first voyage to the New World.

Our journey begins in the snowy stretches of the principality of Moscow, which has just freed itself from Tartar dominion and conquered Novgorod, a very important trading center. From there goods are shipped to the Baltic Sea, and then on to German cities. . . .

Germany

Karl stares at the twin bell towers of the Marienkirche, standing out against the sky with their soaring spires, behind the reassuring mass of the Holstentor, the western gate of the city of Lübeck. In a few months he is going to be married in that church, and the future looks rosy to him. Yet he is anxious to find the answer to a question that has been bothering him for days: Should he give his fiancée two lengths of gold brocade, or enough marten fur to line her ankle-length English wool cloak? Karl must solve this problem before evening, when the solemn engagement ceremonies will begin. Which gift would his future wife like more? He has known her since they were children, because they belong to families of rich merchants who often work together. This is why the choice is so hard for him. The precious gifts he can give her are basically the

same goods his fiancée has already seen in her father's warehouses. Yet she has had a simple upbringing, and her trousseau probably contains no brocades or rare furs, because these are reserved for married women.

Karl thinks it strange to be worrying about such small matters when only a few hours ago he had to supervise the unloading of one ship with a cargo of iron from Sweden and the simultaneous loading of another ship with two thousand pieces of woolen cloth bound for Revel (modern-day Tallinn, in Estonia).

The young man is already an experienced merchant, thanks to his father's training, but he is not unusual. Lübeck is a major trading city, and almost all the men are able traders and feel quite at home amid a variety of merchandise. They are equally skilled at judging the amount of salt needed for a barrel of herring and the quality of dyework in a piece of velvet from Milan.

Lübeck was the first German city to trade in the Baltic Sea and to found other trading settlements along the Baltic coast by colonizing areas inhabited for the most part by Slavic peoples. Even the name of the city is of Slavic origin. Now Lübeck is the queen of the Han-

seatic League. This powerful league, which mercantile towns of northern Germany have formed for the purpose of mutual protection, now controls all trade in the Baltic and North seas. The Hanseatic cities are part of the Holy Roman Empire, but they are free cities, with the right to mint their own currency, make alliances, and declare war. The Holy Roman Empire consists almost entirely of principalities, cities (the largest is Cologne, with about 40,000 inhabitants), counties, and episcopal territories that are virtually independent from the emperor. In 1492 (and for one more year) this is Frederick III, a Hapsburg. The situation in Germany is much like that in Italy, where there are many prosperous separate little states.

Lübeck, which proudly calls itself a "free imperial city," is in a strategic position in the western Baltic. Its port is busy with ships from

1492

Scandinavia loaded with iron, amber, timber, and herring. The eastern Hanseatic ports, situated on the edge of the great Polish-Lithuanian kingdom and the principality of Moscow, handle cargo sold in the Russian town of Novgorod. This includes wax and, most important of all, furs—expensive sable, lynx, beaver, ermine—but there are also spices, silk, and other products from the Far East that arrive via the ancient Viking route to Constantinople. From the Hanseatic port of

1992

Danzig, ships leave with cargoes of wheat grown in the fertile inland plains.

After being unloaded at Lübeck, most of these goods are sent by land to Hamburg to avoid the long and dangerous route around the Danish peninsula. To the west, the Hanseatic trade routes include stopovers in Bruges, London, and along the Atlantic coast of France. Bruges in turn supplies northern Germany with Flemish woolen cloth and luxury items sold by Italian merchants from Genoa, Venice, Florence, and Milan; and London furnishes huge quantities of raw wool and cloth. At the French ports ships pick up enormous cargoes of salt, which is needed to preserve herring (no salt is produced in the Baltic area), as well as wine and other goods from Mediterranean countries.

While it is caught up in this whirlwind of mercantile activity, Lübeck has made itself a city worthy of its prestige and prosperity. The attractive brick houses are solidly built, with typical stepped gables, and the homes of merchants who own ships face the port, so that the famous Hanseatic trading ships land practically on their doorsteps. The city fathers have built a splendid Gothic town hall (the Rathaus, a grand example of medieval German civic architecture), and from time to time they reinforce and repair the city walls and gates. The Holstentor, for example, was finished in the 1470s. Citizens crowd the vast market square, where the many shops offer everything from shoes made of the finest leather to jewelry.

Karl is now going to look in these shops for his fiancée's gift. Even though there are plenty of brocades and furs in his father's warehouses, perhaps he will find something different but equally precious on the counter of some well-stocked shop.

Flanders

After his daily morning walk, Jan turns into
della Borsa Square, pausing a moment to look
around before entering the building where he
works. The town, his beloved Bruges, is already bustling with activity: shops with their
wares on view, merchants and bankers going
to work.

As is his habit, Jan left home quite early. To
protect himself from the cold, damp morning
air he is wearing the warm fur-lined woolen
cloak his mother gave him despite the disap-
proval of his father, who feels this is a dangerous extravagance for a young man. Jan's father
is an official in the city government, a stern,

austere man whose main concern is the future
of Bruges—and for good reason. After centuries of prosperity, this most important mercantile center in Flanders, the major European
port for North Sea shipping, is now becoming
a second-class city. And by a curious stroke of
fate, the decline is due to the two elements that
originally made the city rich—water and
sand.

Bruges was founded in the second half of the

ninth century alongside a river, in an ideal position for trading. The river flows into an arm of the sea that once ran inland among the sandy dunes of the coast; thus ships could anchor quite close to the town. In 1134 a violent storm widened this part of the sea, transforming it into a gulf, the Zwyn, which was only a mile from town and was immediately used as a natural harbor. An outer harbor, the Damme, connected Bruges with the North Sea: goods were unloaded from large ships at the Damme and were then taken on smaller boats to the heart of the city via a system of canals. Gradually the port of Bruges supplanted the traditional fairs of Champagne in France, where trade between Italy and the northern countries depended on land routes; the city became a permanent fair town like Venice and Genoa, where trade took place all year long, not only in certain established periods. Agreements with English royalty made Bruges the center for trading English wool; and this highly prized commodity was exchanged for luxury goods from the Mediter-

ranean, especially silk and spices. Merchants from all over the known world came to Bruges and opened branch offices.

But for more than a century now—and it is this that has been tormenting Jan's father—the town has been fighting a losing battle against the gradual silting up of the Zwyn, which has increased the distance between the town and the sea. Some time ago the outer harbor was moved to Sluis, and new canals have been dug. But in the last few years it has become apparent that nothing can be done against the forces of nature, especially in combination with the political maneuvers of rulers. In 1477, Bruges came under Hapsburg rule when the legitimate heir, Mary of Burgundy, married Maximilian, son of the Hapsburg emperor Frederick III. This couple's heir, Philip (whom everyone calls "the Handsome"), was born in Bruges a year later, and it is said that Max-

1492

imilian intends for his son to marry a Spanish princess to expand the Hapsburg Empire even more. Only four years ago, in 1488, Maximilian asked foreign merchants with branch offices in Bruges to move to Antwerp, and many have done so.

Jan is young, and optimistic about the future, but his father's concern has raised some doubts in his mind. Recently he has been going around Bruges looking for signs of the changes his father mentions. But in becoming acquainted with every nook and cranny of his town, he always ends up being enthralled by it. He is familiar with the views from the many

1992

arched bridges over the canals, the façades of the lovely, solidly built houses with their stepped gables, the impressive palaces, and every inch of the city walls. The tall tower of the city hall, whose octagonal top was completed only ten years ago, seems to him the very symbol of Bruges's greatness. Passing the Hospital of St. John, Jan thinks of the great painter Hans Memling, who since 1465 has produced his masterpieces there, with commissions from rich local patrons. Recently Jan was able to admire one of the master's latest works, *The Shrine of St. Ursula;* its six panels demonstrate the essence of Flemish painting, with its attention to the details of everyday life.

Jan takes a final look at the buildings in which Genoese and Florentine merchants have their offices, and then goes into a building owned by the van der Buers family. Van der Buers is the Flemish name adopted by the della Borsa family, noted merchant-bankers of Venetian origin, and Italian merchants come here to carry out their trade. For this reason the square has an Italian name. Jan's father wants him to become an apprentice accountant in this family's company, so that he can learn all the secrets of international trade and put his gift for foreign languages to good use. Even though Bruges is destined to become a quiet provincial town, Jan can move to Antwerp, where there are plenty of opportunities for the future. After all, Antwerp isn't really so far from Bruges!

England

Thomas is trying to finish his chores quickly. The saddles and horses for the departing guests are ready in the stable, and now he has to put water and firewood in the kitchen. Then he will finally be free to hurry off to see William the shipwright. Thomas can hear the sound of busy axes coming from the shipyard, and he is anxious to see how work on the newest boat is proceeding. The shipyard is very near, but Thomas has not been there in a few days; his parents' inn has been unusually crowded and he has had to help out.

The nearby landing, on the right bank of the Thames just outside London, is used mostly by local people and ordinary merchants, although there is always some pilgrim on the way to or from Canterbury as well. The road

to that town, where the large Gothic cathedral stands, winds inland, and there are many inns along the way. But none of the others, Thomas is sure, offers as tasty a mutton pie as his mother's, her specialty. Perhaps the word has spread, he thinks, and from now on lots of people will come to their inn. He does not like this idea so much, because it means he will not be able to go to the river very often; but he is glad that difficult times are about to end for his family.

Thomas was only five when the thirty-year Wars of the Roses, the civil wars between two factions of noblemen over succession to the throne of England, came to an end in 1485. His father had been the right-hand man for a large, prosperous Cistercian monastery, taking care of the sheep raised by the monks. After he married the daughter of a small land-owner who became involved in the wars out of loyalty to the lord of the region, Thomas's father decided to take his wife and son to London, where life was somewhat safer than in the countryside.

At the beginning of 1486 the Tudor king Henry VII, head of the House of Lancaster (whose symbol was a red rose), married the last descendant of the House of York (whose symbol was a white rose). Peace returned to England, and, with the help of justices of the peace, the king immediately began restoring order in the countryside and limiting the power of the most important noble families. Thomas's parents chose to remain near London, and so they bought the inn. Here the close friendship between the boy and the ship-

wright William developed.

The old man is always willing to explain the secrets of his trade to Thomas—how to choose the right wood (which sometimes comes from as far as Norway), how to chop it and cut it, how to join the planking so that no water seeps in, and so on. For his part, Thomas keeps William up on the latest news and gossip from the traveling guests at the inn. And this morning he has plenty to tell him.

Yesterday evening the boy listened open-mouthed to a description of the exploits of an

1492

archer who had returned from France, where the English made a brief raid (the two countries have been at war for more than 150 years). The soldier showed Thomas his longbow, which can accurately hit a target up to 350 yards away, with arrows about a yard long that can penetrate armor. But a sheep and wool merchant told the bowman that in his opinion firearms would soon become more important than bows and crossbows, and he went on to describe a large cannon used during the Wars of the Roses. Thomas wondered

1992

whether the handsome armor worn by cavalrymen would be of any use against firearms. Recently he saw an Italian suit of armor being taken under armed escort to London to be delivered, it seems, to the king himself.

Yesterday evening too, a group of miners from Devon, on their way back from Canterbury, where they had gone on pilgrimage to give thanks for having survived a mine accident, reported that the cathedral there would soon have a central tower, the gift of Henry VII; teams of bricklayers and stonemasons were already at work. A prelate said that King Henry's second son, who was born last year and named after his father, is a lovely child, the delight of the court ladies; he gives people hope for a long-lasting Tudor dynasty.

An Oxford student who had been listening to the miners took a book out of his traveling bag and began to read by the inn fire. Thomas, who can barely write numbers, looked uncertainly at those pages filled with words. The student told him that if he wanted to learn to read he could ask the parish priest for help. Then he mentioned a certain William Caxton, who died recently, and who in 1477 published the first book printed in England.

Now Thomas wants to relate all these things to his friend William.

France

Now that Martin is among the crowds filling the squares and alleys, he breathes a sigh of relief and wraps himself tightly in his rough student's cloak. He has no lessons this afternoon and wants to enjoy the penetrating March air by wandering around Paris. Martin's family is of modest means, and he managed to get a scholarship to study theology at the University of Paris thanks to the support of a rich prelate in his hometown, Orléans. He knows he is fortunate, because he is free and every day he encounters new, stimulating ideas. But sometimes he feels his lack of money. Today, for example, the meal at the college refectory was meager and tasteless, and he has no desire whatsoever to go back to study in the cold, damp room he shares with four other students.

22

Now Martin looks with a touch of envy at the grand Hôtel de Cluny that Jacques d'Amboise, the powerful abbot at Cluny in Burgundy, is having built as his residence for his rare stays in Paris. The outside seems to be finished, but the workmen have not yet completed the inside. Nonetheless, the bustling of servants and maids shows that someone is staying there, probably one of the abbot's distinguished guests—perhaps a prince in exile, or an ambassador, or even the papal legate. An octagonal tower with an external stairway connecting the different stories stands out against the façade of the magnificent palace. Mentally Martin compares it to the smaller tower in the Ducal Palace in Urbino. He saw that royal Italian residence in a drawing made by a lucky fellow student who had gone on a trip to Italy. Martin saw other drawings by the same student, of palaces and churches in Florence and other Italian cities, and he realized that on the other side of the Alps architecture has taken a different direction from French architecture. Italian architects, who have never liked the vertical thrust of the French Gothic style, are returning to models of classical Greek and Roman architecture with simple lines and forms on a human scale—as in the large windows and "round" arcades (that is, arcades that end in a semicircular arch). Although Martin is struck by these new developments, in his heart he is deeply attached to his country's architectural heritage. In France

the loveliest churches—veritable forests of stone whose upward thrust toward the sky is supported by mighty flying buttresses—date back at least two hundred years. In the early fourteenth century a series of wars against the English (collectively called the Hundred Years' War) interrupted all building, and when it was resumed, the master builders took the past age as their model.

The Hundred Years' War ended in 1453,

1492

24

but it is still fresh in the French people's memory. Even Martin, who is only twenty, knows all about it from what his family told him. He could relate the liberation of Orléans in 1429 under Joan of Arc; he could also describe in detail (because this was his grandparents' experience) the miserable life of the peasants, threatened by enemy troops as well as by roving marauders.

But all this belongs to the past. Now the French kingdom, ruled by Charles VIII, is larger and stronger. Since 1477 it has included Burgundy, though not the entire duchy; Flanders, Franche-Comté, and Artois are under Hapsburg rule. And since 1488 the rebellious duchy of Brittany has been part of the kingdom; in 1491, a year ago, King Charles married the heiress to the duchy, fifteen-year-old Anne. France is about to become a great unified nation, a true international power. Even

1992

though for the time being the king prefers to live in castles of the Loire Valley, Paris will be the heart of this nation.

During his walk, Martin takes in the most obvious signs of new prosperity. The city is more crowded, and the shops offer all kinds of merchandise, even the most expensive. The middle class is becoming richer and richer; they show off their clothes trimmed with rare furs from distant, mysterious lands beyond the Danube.

With the Hôtel de Cluny behind him, Martin walks by the Church of St.-Séverin, which is also in the final stages of construction. Then he crosses over the Petit Pont (Little Bridge), leaving the left bank of the Seine River, where the Université is located, and passes through the Île de la Cité, an island that is the most ancient part of Paris, with the marvelous Cathedral of Notre Dame. He arrives at the right bank, where the city government and various guild houses are found.

The inhabitants of the right bank are not particularly fond of the university students, who come in the thousands from all parts of Europe to this ancient, renowned center of studies. Often there are bloody brawls. But the university nurtures some of the most open and forward-looking minds in Europe. In a few years Martin will have the privilege of meeting Desiderius Erasmus of Rotterdam, who is destined to become one of the leading humanists, those men of culture who are breaking the bonds imposed on humanity by medieval thought.

The Ottoman Empire

Sa'adi is doing rather well at his new job as a stable groom. Because of his age he had to leave his cavalry post, but he is quite happy about working in the stables, since it is the only way he can still make himself useful to the imperial troops. Sa'adi is sixty years old, and at that age he should perhaps think about retiring. But where could he go, and what could he do? He has no family, so he prefers to breathe the dust of military camps, where everything is familiar to him and he knows exactly what to do every moment of the day.

Now it is almost twilight. Soon the last platoon of cavalrymen will end their gallop in the plains and return to the entrenched camp in time for evening prayers. In this little camp on the hill, well guarded by armed sentinels, the pasha of Rumelia (the ruler of European territories conquered by the Ottoman Turks) is waiting for his top-ranking officers to give their daily reports. Then he will dine with the women in his harem, whom he brought with him in covered wagons on his visit to the northern garrisons. The nearby Hungarian border marks the northernmost point between the Ottoman Empire and the rest of Europe, which for decades has been raided by the sultan's troops.

Naturally Sa'adi thinks that the sultan's aims are both just and holy. Now that the Arabs have become weak, it is up to the Turks to establish their dominion throughout the Mediterranean and Europe and bring the true faith of the prophet Muhammad to the Christian countries considered by many to be evil and corrupt. It is in order to take part in this *jihad,* or holy war, that Sa'adi has fought for so long and will now stay in the army as a humble groom.

For the old soldier, life in the garrison basically means tranquillity. He can hardly remember the details of all the battles he has been in during more than forty years of military service. When he was sixteen, in 1448, he fought against the Hungarian cavalry led by John Hunyadi, which had crossed the Danube. In 1453 he was among the troops of Sultan Muhammad II (who was the same age as Sa'adi—twenty-one) during the siege and conquest of Constantinople, the only remaining part of the Byzantine Empire. Sa'adi remembers the fire coming from enormous cannons that hurled balls weighing more than 800 pounds at the city walls; and the strain of transporting seventy biremes overland on greased wooden rollers from the Bosporus to the Golden Horn, to surround the city; and the final assault on the morning of May 29— and then the slaughter and sacking. Muhammad II, from then on called "the Conqueror,"

ordered a reconciliation, and on May 31 he was already praying in the Basilica of St. Sophia, which had become a mosque.

Sa'adi also remembers defeats, such as the one in 1456 at the hands of the Hungarians and their allies, and those inflicted until 1468 in the Albanian mountains by Iskender Bey, or Skanderbeg, the Albanian prince who allied himself with the Venetians and Hungarians. Then there were victorious campaigns and

1492

28

new conquests in the east, all the way to the Crimea. In 1478 Muhammad II's troops were almost at the gates of Venice, when that powerful republic decided it was wiser to pay an annual tribute to the sultan than to fight him. Once again, in 1479, the Hungarians, led by Matthias Corvinus, managed to thwart the Turkish offensive. The following year Sa'adi was among the troops who occupied Otranto in Italy, which was then abandoned in 1481. In the meantime the Conqueror had died and, thanks to the support of the Janissaries, his son Beyazid II became the ruler.

Like all subjects of the Ottoman Empire, Sa'adi has to obey the sultan, but he has always fought as a free man brought up in the Muslim faith. He did his duty in the regular Turkish troops, which consist mostly of cavalry units. The men of this famous cavalry are able to fight at full gallop while wielding a lance and a bow—a skill they inherited from

1992

their distant nomadic ancestors who had roamed through central Asia. Besides the regular cavalry, there are other units: the provincial *siphai*, cavalrymen with estates, who are sometimes Christians; and the palace *siphai*, who are the sultan's slaves. The infantry is made up almost entirely of Janissaries, an elite corps of war captives and slaves of Christian origin taken from their families while still very young and then brought up as Muslims. The Janissaries, as the sultan's personal guard, occupy the central position in the Ottoman army formation in order to protect him, while the various cavalry corps make up the wings.

Everyone, including Sa'adi, is afraid of the Janissaries. He saw them in action at Constantinople and on all the other occasions on which he fought for the sultan. He knows that they are highly skilled in using their scimitars and harquebuses and that they fear nothing, not even the sultan's wrath. They always go into battle shouting "Allah is with us!" but they are often violent and undisciplined, even with the grand vizier, the ministers of state, and high-ranking officers. If something does not go their way, an uprising is likely in the Janissaries' barracks (where they are permanently stationed, since they are not allowed to marry); a revolt is signaled by someone overturning the huge soup pot in the mess. At times it appears that rather than being the sultan's personal guard they are the true rulers in the imperial palace.

Genoa

From the large window in her room Lucia looks down at the sea; she cannot see the Lanterna, the lighthouse that marks the western entry to the port, but she can see the work being done to extend the wharf that stretches out into the gulf in the east, dominated by another lighthouse.

Lucia is meditating. She is quite familiar with Genoa, because she often goes out secretly with her nurse to attend church or wander among the stalls in the marketplace and in craftsmen's workshops. She knows all the city's arcades, and the houses of the Doria family, which, like so many other buildings in Genoa, feature bands of black and white stone. She is acquainted with the lively port

and the road that goes up toward the hills where her family has a house that lies isolated among grapevines and olive trees. She even knows the fishermen's suburb of San Pier d'Arena, the shipyards, and the wool merchants' neighborhood.

But Lucia has never seen her town from the sea, and she almost envies her mother, who arrived in Genoa twenty-three years ago on board a ship belonging to her grandfather, one of the richest merchants in the city. Lucia's father was also on that ship. He was twenty years old at the time, and in Tunis, where he had been called to take care of some business for his father, he fell in love with a fifteen-year-old from Catania who had been kidnapped by pirates. Lucia's father himself paid the ransom

and freed the girl, who became his wife.

Lucia wants so much to travel, to go on long voyages like her brother Bartolomeo, who is twenty-two and has already sailed to faraway places for their father, just as their father once navigated for their grandfather. The family has business interests throughout the Mediterranean, including Spain, and in Portugal too. It deals in all kinds of commodities, and is active in shipbuilding and finance, lending money to private citizens as well as the Republic of Genoa and foreign rulers. Lucia's other brother, Giuliano, also sees to some of the family's business affairs, and he is only eighteen! He is given the shorter, easier journeys; just now the family is expecting his return from Civitavecchia, a port in papal territory where he has gone to pick up a load of alum from the nearby deposits at Tolfa. Alum is used in dyeing cloth and yarn, one of Genoa's most important industries.

Since Lucia is not allowed to travel, she asks her father and brothers to tell her about their journeys. And since she is the baby of the family, they humor her; after all, she is only eleven. So this young girl who has never been out of Genoa can describe Corsica (which is part of the Republic of Genoa), the Balearic Islands, and Seville; she knows that in Lisbon the people speak with an accent similar to that of the Genoese, and that the loveliest linen tablecloths—the ones her mother takes out of the lavender-scented chests on special occasions—come from distant Flanders, in the north. She has told her nurse all about the castle in Naples built by the Aragonese kings, and has described to her the lively ports in Sicily from which wheat and wine are shipped to all parts of Italy. She knows that in the ports of Syria you can find anything you would want from the East, including those beautiful silk or light woolen shawls her mother treasures so much; and that on the island of Chios (where, as Giuliano told her, the Greek poet Homer was born, and which, after being a Genoese possession for more than two centuries, is now being menaced by the Turks), the small mastic trees contain precious resin; and that at Constantinople, conquered by the Turks some forty years ago, people wear slippers with the tips pointing upward.

Lucia knows that Genoa has always been a rival of Venice, the other great Italian sea power, but that this has not prevented the

1492

32

people of the two republics from doing profit-able business with each other. Once a Vene-tian merchant, a guest of her father's, admired her auburn hair and, in that mellow Venetian manner of speaking, so similar to Spanish,

1992

told her that in order to have hair that color Venetian ladies sit in the sun wearing broad-brimmed hats without a crown; these protect their faces and at the same time leave their hair exposed to the sun's rays.

There are some things that Lucia does not understand very well, however. One day she heard her father speaking about a certain Lorenzo the Magnificent as the person who "keeps things in balance." She asked Bar-tolomeo to explain this, and he told her that this was Lorenzo de' Medici, the ruler of Flor-ence for more than twenty years; and the bal-ance he guarantees is the difficult one established among the various Italian states, large and small, so that they do not fight among themselves to the advantage of foreign powers. Because of internal strife among its most important families, Genoa itself has had to accept the "benevolent" protection of the powerful Sforza family ruling in Milan. To cheer her up, Bartolomeo tells his little sister that for years a great Florentine artist, Leonardo da Vinci, has been working in Milan and that—who knows?—he might even come to Genoa one day to organize one of the feasts that have made him so popular and famous at the Milanese court.

Lucia gazes at the sea ruffled by early April breezes and thinks about Milan, Florence, and Lorenzo de' Medici. She hopes that the Mag-nificent will live forever to maintain peace in Italy. She is not aware that in a few days he will die, that in two years French troops will in-vade Italy, and that only in 1528 will Admiral Andrea Doria guarantee Genoa's freedom.

Portugal

The oceangoing ship sails proudly down the Tagus River estuary. Lisbon has been left behind, and in a short time the vessel will reach the ocean. Henrique, a cabin boy, leans on the side of the ship and watches the last stretches of land of his beloved Estremadura pass behind him, the villages shining in the bright, clear morning light. How many months or years will pass before he can once again see those roofs? How long before he can watch the sails of the windmills revolving lazily, or see the restful green of the vineyards and olive groves? The ship he has signed up on is sailing toward the southernmost tip of Africa, the cape that Bartolomeu Dias rounded in 1488 and called the Cape of Storms (later it became known as the Cape of Good Hope). After gradually exploring the coast of West Africa, the Portuguese navigators now want to reach all the waters and lands beyond that cape, as they search for a faster route to the Indies.

Henrique is not afraid of the long voyage, even though he is sorry to leave his mother alone once again. The sea is part of his destiny, just as it was for other members of his family: his father, and his father's father before him. In fact it was his grandfather who wanted to call him Henrique, in memory of Prince Henry (Henrique) the Navigator, King John I's younger son and a staunch believer in the greatness of Portugal, which was to become

powerful not only by acquiring new territories and colonies but also by controlling the most profitable sea trade. Prince Henry died thirty-two years ago, but no sailor has forgotten him, and even this young cabin boy is familiar with his life and achievements.

Henry the Navigator was born in 1394. When he reached adulthood he established his residence in the castle at Sagres, on the cliffs of Cape St. Vincent, the westernmost point of continental Europe. There he set up a base for geographers and navigators, a sort of school to which the boldest youths went to learn the secrets of navigation, and expert sailors (even from such important maritime cities as Venice and Genoa) shared their knowledge and proposed and promoted expeditions along new routes. These feats were achieved with ships much like the one Henrique is now sailing on—caravels and carracks modeled after the oceangoing fishing boats used in northern Europe, but with more space for crew, equipment, and provisions.

Thanks to Prince Henry's men, Portugal colonized Madeira, the Azores, and the Cape Verde Islands and began the methodical exploration of the western coast of Africa, conquering new markets along the way. This enterprising nation also began to explore the interior of Africa, with expeditions to Timbuktu and its treasures. When Prince Henry

died, the responsibility for his great enterprises passed to the Portuguese kings.

The cabin boy named after this great prince is sixteen years old and has been sailing for three years—time enough to get to know almost all the routes followed by Portuguese navigators. He has already been to the Azores, nine islands of volcanic origin in the Atlantic Ocean 900 miles and more from Lisbon. There he followed the flight of the *açôres*, the hawks the archipelago was named after, and in those waters he saw a great many fish— tuna, swordfish, barracuda—and stared with awe at sperm whales spouting huge jets of water. Are these whales the sea monsters that so frighten some sailors? Certainly, young Henrique thinks, whales must not have frightened the ancient sailors who left traces of their presence in the Azores in the form of coins. His captain told him they are Phoenician coins and that the Phoenicians, sailors and

1492

traders who dominated the seas centuries before the rise of the Roman Empire, may even have founded the city of Lisbon.

Henrique has already followed routes to the south as well, calling at Madeira, the base for provisions and a stopping-off point for all Portuguese voyages to Africa. The carrack he is now sailing on will land there before setting off for Guinea, where it will unload merchandise for the local rulers at many ports. The Portuguese have established good, and advantageous, relations with the powerful African realms along the immense Gulf of Guinea.

Henrique learned from his grandfather's accounts that at first sailors were terribly afraid of going south; they thought that along the equator the sea boiled, because of the heat of the sun, and that even if ships managed to pass into the lower part of the earth, they would never be able to return. Then in 1445 a bold captain rounded Cape Verde, and the Por-

tuguese saw the forests of tropical Africa for the first time.

By now the ship is in the Atlantic Ocean, and a harsh voice orders Henrique to get back to his work. He obeys in a flash, and memories, doubts, thoughts, and fears vanish from his mind. He does not know that in a few years, when he will have become an expert sailor, he will take part in Vasco da Gama's great expedition that will finally make Henry the Navigator's dream come true: the route to the Indies and spices. In May 1498 young Henrique will disembark at the Indian port of Calcutta, having sailed around the continent of Africa and crossed the Indian Ocean.

1992

Spain

In the almost unbearable late-morning summer heat, the royal retinue winds through the tilled fields and rocky high ground, leaving clouds of dust in its wake. Joanna turns to Amalia, who is riding just behind her, and the two girls exchange smiles of encouragement. Soon they will arrive at their destination, and the lord of this territory has already prepared everything for the royal couple, Ferdinand of Aragon and Isabella of Castile, and their large train to refresh themselves. This local ruler has built his castle where a caliph's huge villa once stood, and it is said that he preserved the shady inner garden and refreshing fountains so loved by the Arabs.

Amalia is anxious to take off the heavy clothes that her status obliges her to wear, even on a long journey on horseback. A short time ago, she became the maid of honor of Joanna, the daughter of the Catholic sovereigns. Joanna and Amalia are the same age, thirteen, and have become fast friends; but Amalia finds court life, with its many rules and ceremonies, hard to bear, and sometimes she misses the free life she had on her father's property. She is an only child, as her mother died of smallpox shortly after her birth and her father never remarried. The king and queen hold Amalia's father in high regard,

since he has always been their faithful subject, and they showed their favor by calling his daughter to their court. They want to make a perfect lady of me, Amalia thinks, a lady worthy of the new, great country of Spain that after centuries of struggle has freed herself entirely of Muslim dominion and has returned to embrace the true faith of Christ our Lord. This is a mature reflection, for Amalia is a cultured girl, although a bit rebellious and impatient. Her father has given her all the care and education normally given to the male heirs of noble families, choosing the best tutors to teach her Latin, science, and history. Amalia has read about the feats of El Cid, the Spanish hero who lived four centuries ago, and she knows all about the *reconquista,* how Spain slowly won back her land from the Arabs, and about the blood that had to be spilled to do this.

Despite the discomfort of this long journey, she is proud to belong to the retinue now approaching its destination, greeted by peasants crowded on both sides of the road. The king and queen have no royal palace; they move from town to town, from castle to castle, and they and their court are supported by

their various hosts and their subjects. This tradition was established so that the Spanish kings could follow the course of the long war against the Moors; it has not been changed, because the last Muslim prince, the lord of Granada, was defeated and driven away only at the beginning of this year.

Amalia looks ahead, over Joanna's shoulder, and catches a glimpse of Queen Isabella riding next to her husband. Amalia greatly admires the queen, a woman of delicate, refined ways who is at the same time capable of using her power without hesitation. When Isabella inherited the throne of Castile, she wanted to govern it quite independently of her husband, Ferdinand, even though she is very much attached to him.

But something is disturbing Amalia. One of her tutors was a wise old Jew who taught her some astronomy and math. The girl now envisions old Ezechiel, his small, lively eyes, his

1492

white beard contrasting with his simple black smock. And she wonders where he is now. Is he standing on some pier of the Guadalquivir River in Seville, among thousands of other Jews waiting to leave?

Queen Isabella recently decided that all the Jews who were not willing to convert to Christianity had to leave Castile. But even converted Jews, called Marranos, have been watched to determine if their conversion is

1992

sincere. In cases of doubt, the Inquisition, the Church court that judges heretics, intervenes. This is why Spanish Jews, who lived for centuries in peace under Arab rule, are now abandoning all their possessions and going to more hospitable places in Africa or in other parts of Europe.

Amalia remembers Ezechiel with fondness and cannot understand what he did to be treated like this. She did not have the courage to ask for an explanation and is now looking for an answer by staring at the queen. In the end she convinces herself that if Isabella has decided to expel Jews from Spain there must be a reason behind it all.

Amalia cannot imagine that an even crueler destiny is lying in wait for Joanna. She will marry Philip, a Hapsburg (called "the Handsome" because of his good looks), in 1496; but she will become a widow ten years later and will go mad with grief. Joanna will not even understand that her son, Charles, will become king of Spain and of all the territories conquered in North and South America, as well as Holy Roman Emperor.

Now the royal party is in front of the castle. Joanna moves next to Amalia and says: "Do you know that the foreigner, Christopher Columbus, will leave in a few days? If he comes back with treasures we can help the pope reconquer the Holy Land. Wouldn't it be wonderful to go to Jerusalem?"

Christopher Columbus and His Dream

It is a hot, quiet night in early August, but at Palos hardly anyone is sleeping. The sailors already on board the *Santa María*, the *Niña*, and the *Pinta*, the three ships that will set off tomorrow morning for unknown waters, are not sleeping. Nor are their relatives, who are torn by mixed feelings: anxiety because their loved ones are leaving for an unknown destination, and hope that they will return rich and be received with honor.

Christopher Columbus is not sleeping either, in his tiny cabin in the *Santa María*. Seated at his table, he is studying for the thousandth time the maps he has used to plan his voyage, as if this time they might suddenly reveal something new to him. Hours pass, the candle is almost burned out, and Columbus remains seated, waiting for dawn to arrive.

The ocean is only a few miles away, where the Tinto River, on which the port of Palos lies, flows into the Gulf of Cádiz. Columbus can almost smell the ocean air, so different from that of the Mediterranean, not to speak of the sea near Genoa.

Columbus rarely thinks of Genoa, where he was born. He is now forty-one and for more than sixteen years has been living far from that Italian city without missing it at all. His projects were too ambitious for Genoa, which was once powerful and is now torn by internal discord. Here in Spain no one knows anything about his family. Would the king of Portugal and the king and queen of Spain have granted him an audience if they had known he was the son of a modest wool merchant? True, his father had begun to trade more ambitiously, and Christopher, while still an adolescent,

managed to obtain permission to navigate along the Ligurian coast to see to his father's business. Then there were voyages on the high sea, to the coast of Africa and the island of Chios and, when he was twenty-five, to Flanders and England. That voyage was interrupted by a pirate raid, and Columbus saved himself by swimming to safety. He then went to Lisbon, where many Genoese merchants lived.

Now he recalls his eight years in the Portuguese capital, which were so decisive for his future. In Lisbon he worked as a cartographer and soon took up navigating again, first going toward England and Iceland. After marrying a young Portuguese woman from a noble family, he sailed the Atlantic to Madeira, the Azores, the Cape Verde Islands, and the coast of Africa, and then up to the mouth of the Niger River. He learned whatever secrets of the ocean he could on these voyages, and read the most authoritative texts on geography, and talked to sailors and scholars. Slowly but surely the idea of reaching the Orient via a westward route took shape in his mind. Columbus first showed his plan to the king of Portugal, but the idea was rejected. After his

wife died, Columbus moved with his young son, Diego, to Spain, where he had important contacts and friends.

Columbus's memories now turn to more recent events—the long evenings of conversation with the Franciscan monks at Palos who helped introduce him to people who could present him at the Spanish court. His mind goes back to the meeting he finally obtained with the Spanish sovereigns in May 1486, the kind interest shown by Queen Isabella, and then the long wait for an answer that was always delayed (and often impeded by the mistrust of many Spanish scholars) with the excuse that priority was to be given to the reconquest of Granada rather than to the Atlantic voyages.

Finally, on April 17, 1492—only three and a half months ago—in the field of Santafé near

liberated Granada, Queen Isabella and King Ferdinand authorized Columbus to undertake the voyage, assuring him of all the necessary means to organize it. And now it is time to depart, cross the ocean, and land in the Indies and fabulous Cathay (China), described by Marco Polo two centuries ago, and legendary Cipango (Japan), where no European has ever been.

Columbus is sure that in those lands he will find piles of gold, silk, precious stones, and spices. Haven't these same goods been arriving for centuries on the Mediterranean coasts after long and exhausting journeys along the

caravan routes? Conquests of the Ottoman Empire cut off communication with the distant Orient years ago, and now these precious commodities arrive in Europe only through contacts with Arab merchants and mediators.

Yes, Columbus is firmly convinced that his dream will come true: he will see the golden roofs of Cathay; he will manage to conquer new lands and souls in the name of the Spanish crown and Christianity; he will establish fruitful trade relations with the most advanced Oriental nations—and all this will make him and his children, and his sailors and their families, very rich.

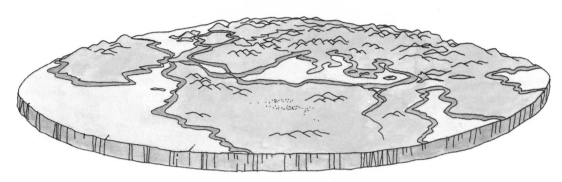

The Geographic Theories

Night is about to end, and soon the crew will start their final maneuvers. Columbus passes his hand over the map spread out on his table. How many discussions and disputes he had with the scholars at the court and at the university in Salamanca because of this map! Here is Europe connected to Asia and, beyond the Mediterranean, Africa, the western and southern coasts of which are being explored by Portuguese navigators. Between the westernmost tip of Europe and Cipango, the easternmost point of Asia, is a long stretch of narrow ocean studded with islands, a sea Columbus is certain he can cross in a few days. This is his concept of the world, the basis of his enterprise. And it is quite erroneous.

Christopher Columbus, like all navigators of his time, knew from direct experience that the earth is round; scholars and all well-educated people knew this too, thanks to the calculations made by ancient Greek astronomers. The old idea of a flat world made up of a mass of known land surrounded by the great stream Oceanus, was now believed only by uneducated people and by those still locked in the Middle Ages, during which many achievements of classical science were forgotten.

In the third century B.C. the Greek mathematician and astronomer Eratosthenes had calculated the earth's circumference, and had come very close to the estimations of modern-day science. Ptolemy, another Greek scientist, in the second century after Christ conceived of a system in which the earth stayed motionless in the center of the universe, while all the other planets and the sun revolved around it. (Some time after Columbus's great discoveries, the Polish astronomer Nicolaus Copernicus replaced Ptolemy's system with one in which all the planets, including the earth, revolve around the sun.) Ptolemy also believed that all the earth's land masses were connected on one half of the globe. Maps based on his system showed Africa joined to Asia by a long strip of land that closed off the Indian Ocean to the south, and made of this body of water an enormous lake. The other half of the earth consisted of a boundless ocean that was impossible to cross.

But Columbus had different ideas. His voyages in the Atlantic had convinced him that the ocean was not so large, was not populated by sea monsters, and could be mastered. So he began to study the works of ancient and modern geographers (as well as the Bible) to find all the hypotheses that agreed with his beliefs.

The papers of the Florentine scholar Paolo del Pozzo Toscanelli (who died in 1482), which Columbus consulted in Lisbon, spoke of Cipango, and this mention brought the Far East even closer to the Iberian peninsula. Toscanelli also stated that Antillia, a mythical land created by the medieval imagination, was

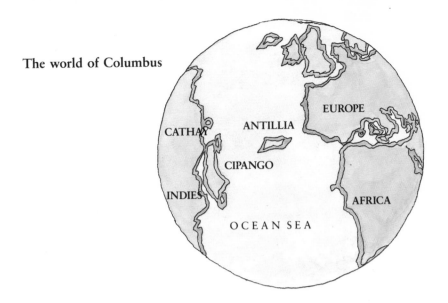

The world of Columbus

in the middle of Oceanus. Columbus believed in the existence of this island, and thought it would be an ideal stopover during the ocean crossing. He "adjusted" his calculations to fit his vision and concluded that the earth's land-masses took up six-sevenths of its surface, while only one-seventh consisted of water. And since the overland distance between Eu-rope and Asia had been known from the time of Marco Polo's journeys, the distance over the sea must be much shorter.

What Columbus's calculations actually did was to make the earth smaller, reducing it to one-fourth of its real size. And with these erroneous measurements firmly planted in his mind, he prepared to embark.

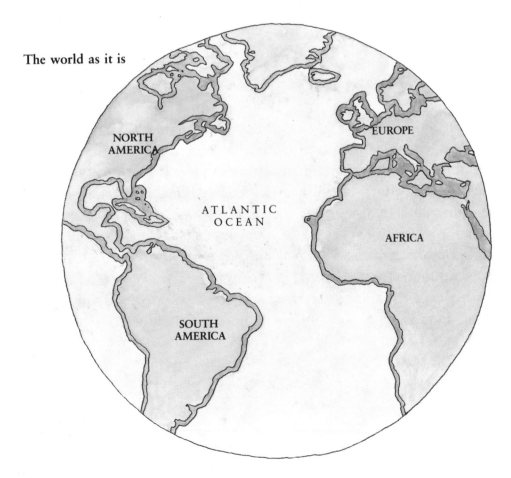

The world as it is

The Ships and the Voyage

The sun has risen. The Admiral of the Ocean Sea—this was the title Queen Isabella and King Ferdinand had conferred on Columbus—is on deck, carefully observing his fleet, and all the men are at their stations ready to carry out the order to sail.

The *Niña* and the *Pinta* are caravels—fast, easily maneuverable sailing vessels about twenty yards long with a rather shallow draft. The *Santa María,* the flagship, is more an oceangoing ship than a caravel, with a greater draft and higher bulwarks; about twenty-four yards long, it is rather squat and not very fast-moving, but is quite suitable for sailing in the open sea. The *Niña* and *Pinta* have been provisioned by the city of Palos as payment of a debt to the queen, while the *Santa María* has been hired with the money Columbus obtained from her.

The crews are made up almost entirely of sailors from Palos who have been persuaded

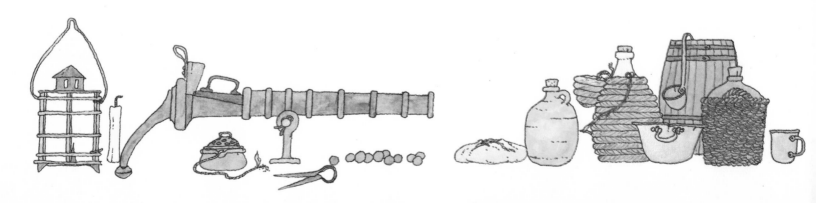

Pinzón, he decides to proceed for a few more days. So the three vessels move on, encouraged by signs that land is near: flocks of birds in flight, branches floating in the water. On Friday, October 12, 1492, the men finally hear the call they have so longed for: "Land ho!"

Columbus gives the name San Salvador to the little island inhabited by peaceful, naked people. He immediately leaves to explore the surrounding area in search of gold, which the natives say is farther south, and sails around the archipelago of the Bahamas, still convinced he is near legendary Cipango.

On October 28, Columbus lands on what is now Cuba and for a while thinks he has arrived at his destination. But there are no cities of gold on that island, as the members of the crew sent to reconnoiter inland report upon their return, and Columbus continues the voyage. The explorers spend the month of November navigating along the coasts of Cuba, and on December 6 they reach another island, which Columbus calls Española (Hispaniola). In the meantime the *Pinta* has disappeared. On December 25 the *Santa María* runs aground on a reef and has to be abandoned. With the help of the natives from the nearby shore the crew manages to salvage some supplies, and the wood of the ship is used to build a stronghold where forty men decide to stay. On January 16, 1493, having found the *Pinta* and explored further, Columbus sails on the *Niña* for Europe.

51

move into the zone of the tradewinds, which blow constantly from east to west, and the voyage now goes at a much faster pace. On September 16 the crews catch sight of floating sargassum seaweed, which Columbus describes as "very green grass" (the area is later named the Sargasso Sea). After twenty days of sailing, the crews begin to complain. The voyage is much longer than they thought it would be, and there are strong headwinds followed by dead calm. In order not to alarm his men Columbus tells them that the distance covered so far is less than he had calculated. On October 6, after meeting with the two captains

to take part in the expedition by their fellow citizen Martín Alonso Pinzón, a famed navigator. He is the captain of the *Pinta,* with her crew of twenty-seven men, and his brother Vicente Yañez Pinzón is captain of the *Niña,* which has twenty-four men on board. Columbus is captain of the flagship, with a crew of thirty-nine sailors. This is a lot of sailors for such small vessels; but they are all necessary, because Columbus has replaced the triangular lateen sails so typical of caravels with square ones that are more suitable for sailing before the wind, and these sails require more men to manage.

The admiral is satisfied with his crews, who are expert at open sea navigation (many sail regularly to and from the Canary Islands, which have belonged to Spain for half a century), used to hard work, and in good health—all requisites for a long voyage on vessels without cabins for the sailors. Instead the holds are filled with equipment and provisions sufficient for one year of navigation. The crews will sleep in the open between watches. The best place to sleep is on the hatch, the trap door leading to the hold; this is the only flat surface of the otherwise slightly arched deck. The sailors' food consists of vegetable soup, salted meat, soaked hardtack, cheese, and pickled sardines; if conditions are good, they will also have fresh fish.

At six in the morning, on August 3, 1492, Columbus has the admiral's ensign raised on the *Santa María* and gives the order to weigh anchor.

After the departure from Palos, Columbus writes down each day's events in his log. On August 8 the ships are within sight of the Canary Islands, where they stop to repair the damaged helm of the *Pinta* and change the sails on the *Niña,* the only vessel that left with lateen sails. Taking advantage of a long stopover, the crew loads more provisions and water on board. On September 6 they enter unknown waters, with the prows pointing due west. After a few days of calm sea the ships

The Return to Spain

On April 20, 1493, Columbus is with King Ferdinand and Queen Isabella in Barcelona and has been honored as a hero. The monarchs listen enraptured to his account of the voyage and his description of the new lands, and they cannot hide their excitement when Columbus shows them the natives he has brought back with him—living proof of his accomplishment, as well as souls to be saved by the Christian faith. He has also brought back parrots, now in cages, whose raucous calls drown out the courtiers' murmuring; and dozens of curious eyes scrutinize the objects Columbus presents to the king and queen: pieces of pure gold (the little he was able to find!), skeins of cotton, amber, multicolored feather headdresses, unknown plants (Columbus often expressed the wish to take a botanist with him). After a thanksgiving Te Deum, Columbus dines with the king and queen. The banquet finally allows him to savor to the full his success and his pride in being a victor. How remote those terrible moments during the return voyage now seem, when he feared he would lose everything he had taken with him, or even die!

The two caravels had to face a rough sea on the more northerly return route, which had been chosen in the hope of finding favorable winds. Between February 12 and 15 the ships were tossed by a violent storm that separated them. The sailors called out to God for help and vowed to make a pilgrimage to the sanctuary of Santa María de Guadalupe, one of the holiest in Spain. After a brief stopover in the Azores, where they were greeted with suspicion by the Portuguese, they once again had to face a storm, and Columbus was forced to land on the Portuguese coast. He left Lisbon on March 13, after being received by King John II. Two days later he landed at Palos aboard the *Niña*. On the same afternoon the *Pinta* arrived; the mid-February storm had driven it north to the Spanish coast on the Bay of Biscay.

Ever since he landed in Spain, great celebrations have been held for Columbus. But only today's, in the presence of the Spanish monarchs, can make up for all those years he spent trying to convince skeptics that his dream was worth pursuing.

The New World

Christopher Columbus has achieved his aim. He is not aware that he has landed in territories not marked on maps, and will not even understand this during his next three voyages. He is convinced he is in the Indies, and thus calls the natives *indios* ("Indians" in Spanish), and he finds them so meek that he tells the Spanish monarchs: "These people are quite inexperienced in handling weapons, and it would take only fifty men to subjugate them all and do whatever one wanted with them." A few years later his words will be taken literally, put to the worst possible use. But in 1492 none of the peoples of North, South, or Central America—except for the Tainos in the Caribbean, whom Columbus first met—is aware of any threat.

From the northern to the southern tip of this vast land many different peoples with different customs live in a wide variety of habitats. Despite their differences, however, they are linked in a way of life that does not use iron. But in areas corresponding to present-day Mexico and Peru, two great civilizations are flourishing—the Aztec and the Inca. The Mayan civilization, on the other hand, which developed in what is now Mexico and Guatemala, is declining.

Our imaginary journey in the year 1492, which began in Europe, will now continue among these peoples, who have a common remote origin. The American continents were populated by successive waves of immigrants from Siberia, starting about 35,000 to 40,000 years ago. At that time, the sea level was lower, because of glaciation; a thin strip of land emerged from the water of the present-day Bering Strait, thus connecting Asia and North America. Asian hunters crossed the strait in pursuit of wild animals, and having found conditions favorable on the other side, they decided to settle.

The Tainos

The bay, usually frequented only by noisy sea-birds and the occasional fisherman, has strangely enough been quite lively since dawn. One at a time, or in small groups, everyone from the nearby village has come to the beach. Guaní, who has carried her little brother in her arms, is among the last to arrive, together with some other girls her age. Young and old alike stare at the sea, their eyes wide with surprise and uneasiness, because before them is something they have never seen until now. Not far from the shore, bobbing on the transparent blue water, is a strange pirogue, as big as one of the village houses. It has no oars, but it has wings! It must be the traveling house of the sky gods that the messengers who came yesterday from a nearby island described. And yesterday evening the village elders met and decided to inform the *cacique,* or tribal chief, who lives in another village not far from here. In the light of the full moon, the fastest youth ran through the thick underbrush, along the path connecting the two villages. When he came back he told the elders that the chief had listened to his news in silence, and merely nodded to the boy to go back home.

Now the chief's large pirogue is approaching in the bay; the *cacique* is sitting calmly under the canopy, as befits a person of his station. He will certainly speak to the un-

known gods who have arrived from afar, Guaní thinks, and will pay homage to them in the most dignified and appropriate way so that no harm will come to the Tainos because of this unexpected visit.

The Tainos are peace-loving people, and although they live on many large and small islands, they have no particular liking for the sea; they hardly fish at all, nor do they hunt very much. Yet the stories handed down from generation to generation narrate how, many centuries ago, they sailed to these islands in their pirogues. With another people of the same stock, the Arawaks, they left their territories in a distant land to the south by traveling down a great river, and in successive waves they occupied almost all the islands in this sea. When a group of Tainos found an island considered suitable, they would settle there and take up their age-old agricultural practices. They would clear a patch of forest by burning the trees, and after spreading the ashes evenly over the earth, they would use pointed sticks to plant the seeds they had carefully preserved on their voyage. After many harvests of corn, beans, and pumpkins had exhausted the earth, they would repeat the same operation in another part of the forest. With time the Tainos learned to make use of local plants as well and to capture edible birds, which, along with some small land animals, were their only source of meat.

For many years the Tainos lived peacefully on the multitude of scattered islands. They became skillful at carving stone, making not only axes and mortars needed to cut plants and grind corn, but also sculptures. From their land of origin they had brought their knowledge of pottery, and they continued to make beautiful vases and graceful figurines. Even wood was elegantly shaped with stone tools. They were skilled at weaving plant fibers—although clothes were practically un-
1492

56

necessary in the warm climate—and knew how to intertwine rope to make hammocks. The Tainos lived in long huts made of branches set over a framework of poles, each hut shared by several related families.

Then one day the Caribs arrived. These people also came from the great lands in the south, but to the north of the big river. They spoke another language and had many different customs. They were hunters and warriors, and they used their lances and bows and arrows with great ability. Above all they were cannibals.

The Caribs would land on the beaches, as if out of nowhere. They killed the men and ate some of them on the spot. Then they left, taking the rest of their "supplies" and the women and children, whose lives were spared so they could become part of the tribe. Despite their love of a quiet life, the Tainos were forced to come up with some kind of defense besides

1992

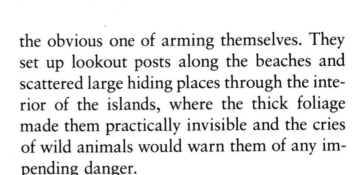

the obvious one of arming themselves. They set up lookout posts along the beaches and scattered large hiding places through the interior of the islands, where the thick foliage made them practically invisible and the cries of wild animals would warn them of any impending danger.

This is why Guaní hopes that the chief will establish good relations with the unknown gods . . . if they are gods. And if they turn out to be marauders even crueler than the Caribs? She shudders at the thought and looks around, taking in the expressions on the faces of her relatives and neighbors. The old people are especially worried and nervously inhale smoke from the slow-burning rolled tobacco leaves.

A sort of pirogue has detached itself from the large floating hut. It is filled with strange men who are making gestures—perhaps of greeting—to the *cacique*'s pirogue and heading for the shore, accompanied by the most daring and curious of the Taino boys, who are swimming alongside their boat. Now the strangers are setting foot on the beach. Their faces are as white as cotton but are partly covered by hair; they are dressed in cloth that covers their entire body, and their chests are enclosed in a sort of shiny turtle shell. A sheath hangs from their hips; it seems to contain a long knife. All the villagers approach slowly. So does Guaní, who cannot help wondering: Are they friends or enemies?

The Aztecs

Ximaltli, an agile thirteen-year-old boy, has managed to find a good spot from which to observe the ceremony that is about to begin. He does not want to miss any of it. Now the prisoners of war are arriving, in lines; soon they will walk one by one up the 104 steps leading to the top of the great pyramid where the twin temples of Tlaloc, the rain god, and Huitzilopochtli, the god of war, stand side by side. On the narrow platform in front of the temples the prisoners will be stretched out on the sacrifice stone, where a priest will then rip open their chests, take out their hearts, and offer them to the gods. Ximaltli knows that because of this sacrifice the gods will grant the Aztec people their protection and will help them become more prosperous and powerful.

Ximaltli is proud of being Aztec. In the military school where he is learning to use weapons, he has also learned the history of his people, who in a few centuries have created a vast empire by conquering nearly all neighboring peoples. When the first Aztecs reached

58

the heart of the Valley of Mexico, they took refuge on the little island of Tenochtitlán, amid the swamp grass and mosquitoes of Lake Texcoco. That island is now the splendid capital of the Aztec empire, a huge city with well-laid-out roads and canals, many fine buildings and temples, marketplaces and residential quarters. On three long embankments, which are interrupted at intervals by bridges for canoes to pass under, are the roads that connect the city with the valley. An aqueduct that begins at the western bank supplies Tenochtitlán with fresh water, because the lake water is salty.

The Aztecs have learned something useful from every population that they have conquered or that disappeared before their arrival. From the Toltecs, they learned to erect mighty stepped pyramids to honor the gods and observe the stars. They have also adopted a Toltec god, Quetzalcoatl, worshipped in the form of a serpent that instead of scales has the wonderful feathers of the quetzal bird. The plumed serpent god does not demand blood, only flowers and butterflies. For some mysterious reason Quetzalcoatl has abandoned his faithful; the priests say that he will return from the east on a predestined day, and will appear as a white man with a beard. This will be a strange apparition to the Aztecs, who have copper-colored skin and hairless faces.

From the Mixtecs the Aztecs have acquired a taste for goldwork. Only the nobles and high officials can wear the splendid gold breast-plates, earrings, necklaces, and other jewelry made by Mixtec goldsmiths. But Ximaltli is not envious. He knows that his people are strong because they are divided into well-organized, clearly distinguished classes. The emperor is the absolute ruler and governs with the help of dignitaries and priests. Each social class has its own precise duties to carry out. Yet those from the humblest classes, and even slaves, have the opportunity to move up the social ladder through personal merit.

Ximaltli now admires the cloak of an im-

1492

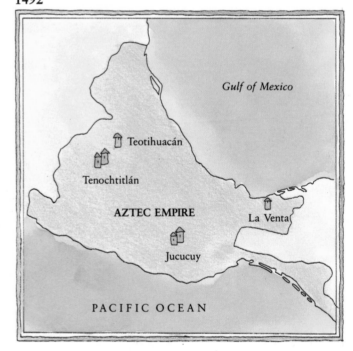

58

portant military leader; its thousands of small multicolored feathers are sewn together with extraordinary skill. Ximaltli hopes to attain a higher social position by becoming a brave warrior. His father is a boatman, and the family's modest brick house lies at the edge of the city, near a stretch of *chinampas,* rafts made of trunks and branches that are anchored to the ground and filled with fertile earth. These rafts are the "kitchen gardens" of Tenochtitlán. Tomatoes, melons, beans, and even trees are grown on them. With time the roots of the plants bind the rafts to the bottom of the lake, creating another landmass that will be added to the city's territory.

Ximaltli wants a house built of stone and stucco, white like the noblemen's palaces and the great pyramid. In order to have such a house he will become a soldier; he will organize armed expeditions and go to the farthest reaches of the Aztec Empire. He will trade salt

1992

and cocoa for gold dust, rubber, jade, turquoise, topaz, quetzal feathers, seeds of rare plants, resin and precious dyes, shells, pearls, and of course obsidian, the volcanic mineral that can be skillfully sharpened to make knives like those that will tear open the chests of the prisoners very soon. All these goods, and many more, are taken to Tenochtitlán as tribute paid by the emperor's subjects to the central government. Some of them go to the ruler and his court, while the rest are sold. But anyone brave enough to seek out the rarest goods where they grow or are produced, and thus face the danger of hostile populations and the long and difficult journey, will almost certainly become rich.

Ximaltli sees two of his friends in the crowd. One will become a sculptor, able to represent the features of the gods in stone; the other will become a scribe, who with paint and reeds will write in the sacred texts made of buckskin and agave paper. Ximaltli calls them, and together the three watch the first prisoner walk up the pyramid stairs.

In 1519, Ximaltli and his friends will see a white man with a beard arrive from the east. He will not be the god Quetzalcoatl returning, as the emperor Moctezuma believes, but the Spanish conquistador Hernán Cortés. In about two years' time the Aztec Empire will collapse: the temples and palaces will be destroyed, the books burned, the gold ornaments melted down. Where Tenochtitlán now stands the Spaniards will found Mexico City.

The Maya

The *balam,* or jaguar, swings on the long pole from which it is hanging. Now that it is tied up, the proud animal no longer frightens anyone. The young hunters searched for a long time in the thick brush of the hot, humid tropical forest, holding their lances upright so that the sharp flint points would protect their heads (jaguars like to sit on the upper branches of trees, ready to leap on their prey). When they found the creature's tracks the hunters set a trap, using a tapir as bait, and finally they captured the big cat. Three Cauac held the jaguar's jaws shut while his companions tied its legs. Now they are taking it to the *chilam,* the old priest who lives alone among the ancient temples of their ancestors. He will decide whether to keep the jaguar in a cage or kill it to use the skin as a sacred mantle.

Three Cauac carefully observes the ruins of the pyramids and the walls of the palaces almost swallowed up by the ferns and lianas. The priest might be in any one of the impressive buildings, because on certain days and at certain times of the year he visits them all to perform a ceremony in honor of the gods. Perhaps they will find him in the temple dedicated to the greatest god of all, Itzamna, the creator of writing and the calendar. Of all the young hunters, only Three Cauac knows

erected new buildings under the supervision of architects, while stonemasons and plasterers decorated the façades and painters made vividly colored frescoes in the temples. The priests ruled the cities according to the will of the gods, and the entire population obeyed them.

But suddenly the orderly and prosperous Maya world fell to pieces. The cities were abandoned, and only small groups of huts remained. The cities in the forest were never inhabited again, while those in the north were invaded by foreign peoples who brought new customs and new gods with them, such as the cruel Kukulcán, who demanded bloody human sacrifices. In those distant cities, the old priest told Three Cauac, the invaders were slowly assimilated by the Maya; but the Maya are no longer the same people as of old. Now they love war, and the caste of noble warriors is almost more important than the priests.

1492

something about the gifts the gods have bestowed on mankind. The old priest spoke of this to him, because he considers Three Cauac the potential heir to the ancient wisdom of their people, the Maya.

The priest explained to the boy that the Maya were once great and powerful. They had built many cities of stone and lime, not only in that forest but in the north as well, where the arid land juts out into the great waters. Each city had tall stepped pyramids crowned by a temple or an observatory to watch the movements of the stars. There were palaces for the priests and nobles, granaries, cisterns to collect rainwater, sacred wells, and fields for ball games. The grassy areas were traversed by *sachés,* paved ceremonial paths used for processions; the gods continually demanded offerings of food and perfumed resin, and less often, human sacrifices. People lived in peace, except for some minor disputes between neighboring towns, and everybody had enough to eat, because almost the entire population tilled the land and harvested the crops, not only for themselves but for priests, government officials, and warriors as well. And when they were not busy in the fields, the peasants

The priest has taught Three Cauac that the earth is a square lying on the back of an enormous caiman; above it are thirteen stars held up by the Bacab, gigantic demigods, while underneath are the nine kingdoms of the gods of darkness. In the center of the earth is a huge green tree, and each of the four cardinal points is marked by a sacred tree of a different color: red for east, white for north, black for west, and yellow for south. The same colors were once used to paint the façades of temples and the masks of Chac, the rain god.

The old priest has also begun to explain to the boy the importance of passing time. Time is a weight carried by the gods, and every day of the year is a different god. There are two Maya calendars; in one, the year is based on the cycle of the sun and consists of eighteen twenty-day months, plus five unlucky days; the other is a 260-day holy year with thirteen twenty-day months. The two calendars coin-

1992

The holy calendar. The symbols for the numerals from 1 to 13 are arranged in the inner circle; the symbols for the twenty days of the month are in the outer one.

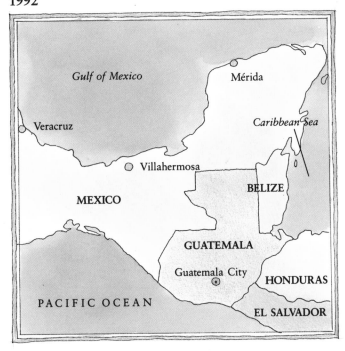

cide (that is, they begin on the same day) every fifty-two solar years, which constitute the Maya "century." The *katun* (twenty-year period) is so important that the ancient Maya built an upright sculpted stone, or stela, at the end of each one. Every day of the holy year is indicated by a combination of one of the twenty names of the day and a number from 1 to 13. Children are given the number and name of the day of their birth, and they also take on the character of that day. Three Cauac, for example, was fortunate: 3 Cauac, his birthday, is under the sign of nobility and makes him worthy of respect.

In the next three years the old priest will teach Three Cauac all the secrets of the ancient Maya. He will learn to read their writing, consisting of ideographs, once carved on stelae and copied by scribes in books made of fig-tree bark. He will also learn to observe and describe the movement of the stars and planets, and to celebrate many rites.

But by now the glorious Maya world is remembered only by a few priests, and in a short time even they will have no more followers. The ancient wisdom of these people will be forgotten forever.

The Inca

The light of dawn gradually reveals an entire city perched on the side of a steep cliff. At the bottom of the precipice pockets of darkness linger over the Urubamba River. On the highest point in the city, in front of the solar rock, the high priest has just finished officiating at a ceremony of greeting for Inti, the sun god. He has thanked Inti for having risen today, bringing another day of life to his people. At the same moment the young messenger Capac leaves the governor's building. Tied to his belt are a small gourd with water and a light cotton bag with the message—all he needs to run several miles. At the relay station he will give the message to another messenger who will run the next stage; Capac will then rest and refresh himself.

The boy runs along paved streets that wind among the high walls of the dwellings; he descends the stairs that connect the different levels of the terraced city and then runs beside the strips of tilled land. Soon, at the end of the longest series of steps cut out of the rock, he will pass through the city gate, go down toward the river and then immediately ascend on the wide, well-laid-out path. Though still young, Capac has been delivering messages for a year and has ventured quite far from his city on the cliff. But he can't say—as the older messengers do—that he knows every corner of the immense empire ruled by the *inka*, Tupac Yupanqui, who is the incarnation of the sun god.

In the course of a hundred years the divine Inca imperial family has conquered more and more territories, extending its dominion in

The Andes populations have no paper or written language; but they have an ingenious numbering system that uses strings, called *quipus,* for keeping accounts and recording events. The strings, of various colors and sizes, are knotted in different ways and attached to a cord. The *quipu* Capac has in his bag indicates the population of the town he has just left as well as the quantity of agricultural products that must be consigned to the *inka*.

Along his path Capac meets one of the many llama caravans from the highest areas of a plateau where there are no trees or tilled fields. Such caravans descend with loads of rock salt, hides, and vicuña wool, then return with goods from the lowlands—potatoes, beans, peppers, rice, coca leaves, and firewood (but not corn, which is the food of the gods and is reserved for the *inka* and his family). The caravans from the little islands along the coast bring that fine fertilizer produced by seabirds,

1492

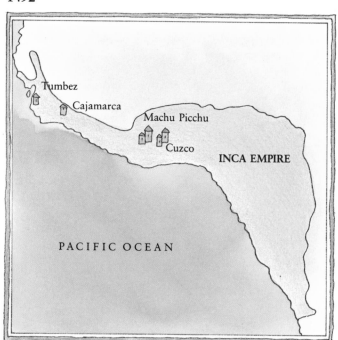

every direction from Cuzco, the center and capital. The *inka* is the absolute ruler. He uses the powerful caste of priests, who are his relatives, to oversee government officials and soldiers. Every family has its own house and an area of tillable land, or the tools needed for its trade, but two-thirds of the cultivated land belongs to the emperor and is worked by his subjects for no pay. Since rainfall is very scarce, a system of canals is needed to irrigate the fields. Two main roads cross the vast empire from north to south, one along the coast and the other, the "royal way," over the mountains. These roads are connected by numerous crossroads and suspended bridges made of interwoven lianas and wood that sometimes pass over precipices. The bridges are used by bearers, warriors, government officials, priests, and above all by the messengers who must regularly take local officials' reports to Cuzco.

guano, to the agricultural regions.

As he runs, Capac thinks of Cuzco. He has seen the capital only once, and was dazzled by it. From the central plaza—which according to the ancient sages is the center of the world—four roads move out toward the four regions of the Inca Empire: Chinchasuyu (the northwest), Cuntisuyu (the southwest), Antisuyu (the northeast), and Collasuyu (the southeast). All homes are in buildings that surround large inner courtyards, and each group of buildings is located inside a walled-off zone with only one entrance gate. Each of these "blocks" contains families descended from the same ancestors. The walls of the most important buildings gleam with the gilding over the stone. Capac was not able to visit the Coricancha quarter, the "golden enclosure," because people of his class are not allowed there; but he has heard descriptions of it. In the temple of the sun there is a large golden disk

1992

representing the sun god; at certain times of the day, when the sun's rays hit this disk, it shines as if Inti had actually descended to the earth. The inside walls of the temple garden are covered with gold leaf and have life-size reproductions of plants, animals, and men in gold and silver. The skilled goldsmiths who created these figures are Chimus—people of the last civilization conquered by the *inka*. It is they who make the funeral masks that cover the mummies of the rulers, as well as the jewels for the nobles and ceremonial knives.

Capac knows he will never have those symbols of wealth and power as a humble messenger boy. His life will be dedicated to serving the emperor. What he does not know is that in some forty years gold will be the cause of the destruction of his people's civilization. The flocks of llamas, the four hundred varieties of potatoes, the hard labor of the peasants, and the ruins of imposing walls will be all that remains of the great Inca Empire.

69

The Buffalo Hunters

It is almost sunset; the summer evening is calm and warm. At the fires in front of the tepees, the women are roasting buffalo meat. Deerfoot leaves the group of youngsters running from one end of the camp to the other, still excited by the hunt; he prefers to stand by the fire and smell the cooking meat. He is thinking that his friends will make fun of him—almost old enough to become a warrior, here he is among the squaws, like a little boy!

But the real reason he is by the fire is that this is the only place he can avoid the smell of blood coming from the soaked earth, from the skinned carcasses and the hides already hanging on poles to dry. Deerfoot has a very keen sense of smell, exceptional even for the people of his tribe—the Mandans, hunters, farmers,

and warriors living on the Great Plains—who have always relied on their sharp senses to survive in this boundless territory. Their land has an abundance of food but is also fraught with danger in the form of nature and hostile tribes. "We should have named you Buffalo Nose," his father once told him. But that sensitive nose, which in a few years will help him hunt and "sense" the presence of enemies, now only torments him with the odor of buffalo blood. . . .

While waiting for his portion of roast meat, Deerfoot goes over the events of the last few days and hours. He can still hear the thunderous trampling of the buffalo running toward the trap the tribe set for them, the men shouting to frighten them and direct them

70

1992

toward a gorge, and the furious barking of the dogs. Everything had been planned very carefully: first of all choosing the site, a hilly area on the northeastern edge of the plains, ideal because of the many gorges; then setting up camp a short distance from the bottom of the precipice chosen as the trap; and last, finding the herd to be hunted.

Two evenings ago the men held a meeting to decide the strategy for the hunt. Yesterday evening there was a propitiatory dance, a sort of simulated battle between the hunters and the animals, the latter impersonated by men wearing buffalo heads. And this morning at dawn the hunt began. The herd selected for the hunt was outflanked and almost surrounded. The hunters crawled toward the buf-

falo downwind; they wore fresh buffalo hides, because these animals, with an even keener sense of smell than Deerfoot's, can detect the odor of humans from far away. The women, children, and adolescent boys—including Deerfoot—who are not allowed to take part in the hunt, watched silently from a nearby stretch of high ground. Everything was quiet. Then the men shouted all together and the herd, skillfully directed by the hunters, began to run toward the gorge. The buffalo fell headlong down the rocky ravine, where the hunters finished them off with bows and arrows and axes. The boys and women helped drag the carcasses to the camp, and for the rest of the day the entire tribe was busy skinning and cutting the huge beasts.

The Mandans use every part of the buffalo they catch. The meat not eaten fresh is dried for the winter; the hide is transformed into tepees, boats, blankets, and moccasin soles;

1492

the mane and tail hair is twisted into strong cord; the bones become arrowheads, needles, and other useful objects; and perhaps some hardy warrior will convert the powerful horns into a bow. Buffalo will be hunted until the tribe has all it can carry with it. To return from the grassy summer hunting areas to the wooded winter lands where they have fields of corn and tobacco, the Mandans must walk for days.

If the buffalo did not go south during the winter, Deerfoot thinks, toboggans could be used for transport, since they carry a much larger load. The round earthen dwellings in the winter village are spacious, each accom-

1992

modating a family and its possessions, and dozens of people besides. It would really be comfortable, Deerfoot reflects, to have soft hides spread all over the floor, not just where they sleep.

His mother hands him a piece of meat, and Deerfoot looks around while chewing on it. A splendid white-feathered peace pipe is being handed around among a group of elders seated in a circle. A young warrior, so proud of the eagle feather that has recently been put in his hair, plays the flute for a girl wearing a dress of soft deerskin decorated with porcupine needles and colored patterns. The boy's bare chest carries the scars from the trial of endurance and courage he underwent, during which he remained hanging for hours by ropes tied to large pegs attached to his flesh.

Now the shaman moves toward the center of the camp. Of all the men in the tribe, he is the one who has the most extraordinary visions and dreams; he is able to foresee the future and cure diseases. He will now do a solo dance to thank the invisible, all-present spirit that protects the tribe, and afterward everyone will sing and dance through the night.

Yes, Deerfoot thinks, this is a great day!

The Villages Under a Rock Roof

Seated with his legs crossed and his back against the still warm rock, Two Feathers observes the narrow valley far below. From a few yards overhead he hears the buzzing activity as the villagers do their final chores before dusk arrives and the evening fires are lit. Most of the corn has been harvested. All day, men, women, and children have gone back and forth along the steep path connecting the village to the cornfields in the valley, and now the cobs are lying on the roofs of the houses, many already husked. Some of the women are now hurrying to fill their terra-cotta pitchers at the spring that gushes out of the rock wall.

The high priests as Two Feathers knows, are meeting to discuss whether to abandon the village their ancestors built under the rock on the mesa, and erect another one next to the farmland in the valley. Meanwhile the rest of the villagers continue with their daily tasks. This does not mean they are unconcerned; they are well aware this would be a drastic change. But they are Hopis, by nature a reserved, peaceful, moderate people who are neither too curious nor too emotional. If the priests decide to remain in this village, everything will go on as before; if, as is probable,

they decide to move, the families will leave their centuries-old village without too much regret—as have other Hopis before them, and other tribes with a different language but a similar life-style, such as the Zunis.

Two Feathers' grandmother told him why, long, long ago, their ancestors decided to settle in the natural shelter offered by the smooth wall of rock that rises up in the mesa overlooking the river. Their people had lived in peace for a long time in the valleys below, in dwellings made of rock and adobe; they had learned to grow corn, beans, and cotton in the rather arid land. Then the Apaches arrived from the north with their powerful bows. There were many minor skirmishes and no safety and order until the newcomers finally settled in neighboring areas. In the meantime, the Hopi built fortified villages on the foothills or took refuge on the faces of the cliffs.

Sometimes the Apaches come to Two Feathers' village to trade; in exchange for cotton, corn, and rabbit skins they bring turquoise and colorful feathers of birds from distant lands beyond the desert (actually they are parrot feathers that come from Mexico through a series of trades). Two Feathers compares the Apaches with his people. They love war and plunder, he thinks, although we have taught them to till the soil. We Hopis try never to kill, and if we must kill, only the members of the warrior clan are allowed to do so, after purifying themselves through isolation and various ceremonies. The Apaches build crude huts of branches and earth. Our houses are square, placed next to one another, and the rooms are built over one another so all the women from the same family can live together with their mother (or even their grandmother) and with their husband and children. The Apaches always hope to become chiefs, whereas none of us wants to be more important than anyone else. The Apaches have shamans and sorcerers, while we have priests whose only concern is to officiate at religious ceremonies as correctly as possible. Since we have so many rites, the people chosen as priests are those who know these rites best. The Apaches cut off the nose of a wife who has betrayed her husband, and allow a man to have more than one wife. In our tribe any disagreement between husband and wife is solved peacefully through divorce, and a man is allowed only one wife at a time. Before being considered adults, Apache boys must go through hard and painful initiation rites. We must go through

1492

76

only a brief ceremony in the kiva, the underground chamber used for religious purposes. During this ceremony we learn that the kachina gods are really only the village men in masks; we promise never to reveal this secret and are admitted into the adult world.

This reminds Two Feathers that he can no longer act like a child and remain alone with his thoughts while the whole village is busy at work. He has already gone through the initiation ceremony in the kiva, and next year he will take part in the Snake Dance for the first time; he must behave like all other adult Hopis. He already knows how to till the land and sow seeds, hunt deer and rabbits, and weave. He still has a lot to learn about making jewels out of colored stones, turtle shells, and other shells; and he must learn how to decorate his ceremonial mask with brushes and paint and how to use colored sand to make the ritual paintings on the floor of the kiva. He would also like to be able to weave baskets, make pottery, and help build new houses, but these activities are reserved for women; and good Hopi that he is, Two Feathers is not disappointed about this.

1992

The Lake and Forest Tribes

Seeing all that activity onshore, Duck Eye, one of the youngest girls in the village, cannot help thinking that the old sachem was right once again: last winter he suggested that the tribe move to a territory he had explored during his youth. There they would find plenty of game and fish because no one, not even other Algonquin tribes, had ever been there. But most important, they would be more secure from the threat of their main enemies, the Iroquois.

The tribe had listened carefully to the old man's words; they respected his wisdom and expertise, and knew his abilities as a great hunter and fisherman. Then they all freely discussed his idea and the majority agreed with him. So when better weather arrived they abandoned the old village, and after a long trip, partly on foot and partly by canoe, they arrived in this secluded corner of the forest where a quiet river descends and flows into a large lake. The men immediately felled pine

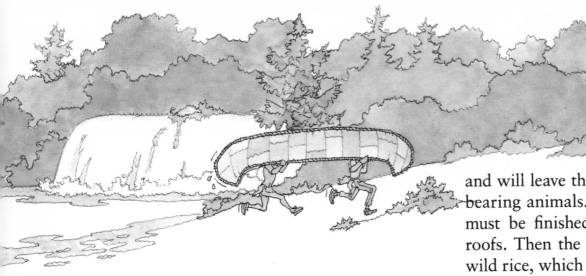

trees with their stone axes and built a sturdy round palisade with a single entrance. They erected huts in this well-protected enclosure in just a few days, and once this work was finished, the tribe went about its usual daily tasks.

Duck Eye looks around and sees the skillful canoe-makers at work replacing the boats that were lost or ruined during the long trip. On a framework of cedar branches curved and then tied together with strips of animal skin, they fasten the rolls of birchbark, whose ends are carefully joined; they then waterproof the surface by varnishing it with a mixture of resin and animal fat. These canoes are light and can be carried easily should the tribe meet with rapids too difficult to navigate or have to take a land route from one lake to another. But the canoes are also fragile, and some tribesmen prefer leather to birchbark because it is more resistant to hard impacts.

The village women have set fillets of *namaycush,* or lake trout, on racks to dry; once the fish is ready it will be put in wooden boxes and set aside for the winter. Pemmican, dried meat powder mixed with fat, is also eaten in the winter. In summertime, on the other hand, the tribe prefers to eat fresh fish and meat, so the fishermen and hunters are kept busy.

Duck Eye knows there is a lot to be done to prepare for the cold season. When it snows, the men will put wooden frames on their feet

and will leave the village to set traps for fur-bearing animals. Before that time the houses must be finished with birchbark walls and roofs. Then the villagers have to harvest the wild rice, which grows along the shores of all the lakes in this area. Duck Eye took part in last year's harvest with the other women. Seated in canoes, they grasped the stalks of rice and bent them toward the inside of the boat; then they beat the stalks lightly with sticks to remove the rice grains. While they will have rice this year, next winter there will be no maple sugar for the tribe. In order to gather the sweet sap that becomes crystallized sugar when cooked and stirred for a long time, the women should have cut the maple

1492

trunks in April; but this April the tribe was getting ready to move, so they decided to do without maple sugar. Now the oldest tribeswomen are looking for marsh plants good for curing wounds and sores, while Duck Eye and some other children are busy in the woods gathering fruit, one of summer's gifts. Fortunately, nuts and berries can be found near the village; everyone feels safe with lookouts close by to keep watch.

Even in the new village, despite its seclusion and peaceful surroundings, no one has forgotten the Iroquois. They should be far away, but you never know: they are treacherous as snakes and know all the secrets of the waterways and woods, and they might appear at any moment.

Why, Duck Eye wonders, aren't the Iroquois content with the territory they have already conquered, and why don't they leave us in peace? They have plenty of fertile land to

grow many varieties of squash, beans, and corn; they have rivers filled with fish; and then there are the caribou, elk, deer, beavers, ducks, turkeys, and wild pigeons that thrive in their land as well as in ours. Maybe they want to take away our possessions because they consider themselves stronger. But then why are they always at war, even among themselves? No, Duck Eye concludes, they are simply cruel; they love to torture their prisoners before killing them. But this time, if they attack us we will defend ourselves.

A friend interrupts these gloomy thoughts to invite Duck Eye to her home to see her family treasures in secret. In her hut the girl takes a doeskin sack from a pile of tanned hides and skins, and pulls out some splendid wampum beads to show Duck Eye. There is also a belt decorated with little cylindrical shell pearls arranged to recall the course of a river. Then there are other, smaller beads where motifs are merely decorative, with no symbolic meaning. Finally Duck Eye, full of admiration for these precious objects, forgets the Iroquois and asks herself whether Manito, the great spirit in all things, is not also in wampum.

1992

The Admiral's Destiny

A few days after his triumphant meeting with the sovereigns in Barcelona in April 1493, Columbus began planning his next expedition. It took several months to organize: this time he had to cross the ocean with seventeen sailing ships, about 1,200 men, a number of domesticated animals and a large supply of plants and seeds. The monarchs wanted to colonize the new territories, convert the natives, and search for gold. So they sent their own envoy with Columbus.

Columbus's second voyage began on September 25, 1493, from the port of Cádiz; it was to end there some three years later, on June 11, 1496. It accomplished little, and was marred by a series of events that damaged the relationship between Columbus and the sovereigns. During the outward journey, along a more southerly route than in the first journey, Columbus landed on a dozen or so new islands, including Dominica, which was sighted on December 3, and Santa Cruz, the scene of his first armed confrontation in the Caribbean. When he reached Hispaniola, Columbus found the fortress-colony of La Navidad, which had been set up on the first voyage, completely destroyed. He established a new colony nearby and named it Isabella. It was in a marshy area, and the site proved disastrous because of its unhealthy climate.

of what is now Cuba, he became convinced that it was not an island but a peninsula, the Malay Peninsula. His fleet was drastically reduced, as he had sent twelve ships back to Spain to ask for reinforcements, and four others had been lost in a hurricane. With his remaining caravel, the *Niña,* a veteran of the first voyage, and the *India,* which had been built in Hispaniola, loaded with two hundred Spaniards and fifty Tainos, many of whom died during the voyage, he returned to Spain in 1496.

After a less than triumphant return to Cádiz in June, Columbus had to wait until October for an audience with the sovereigns. In Seville, where he was staying, the townspeople called him "Admiral of the Mosquitoes." Isabella and Ferdinand had received complaints about his actions in Hispaniola, but after the audience their confidence in him was restored. He remained in Spain, planning his third voyage, while his brother Bartolomeo governed Hispaniola in his absence.

Columbus's second voyage had rekindled the old rivalry between Spain and Portugal. The two kingdoms asked Pope Alexander VI, the Spaniard Rodrigo Borgia, to establish their areas of influence in the unclaimed territories. After consulting with Columbus, the pope took a map and drew a line 100 leagues west of the Cape Verde Islands. Portugal was given rights to the lands west of the line, and Spain to those east of it. However, the rulers of the two countries met in Tordesillas, Spain, on June 7, 1494, and agreed to move the line 270 leagues farther west.

At the end of May 1498, Columbus left Sanlúcar de Barrameda with six caravels. When the fleet reached the Canary Islands, it split up. Three ships set sail for Hispaniola,

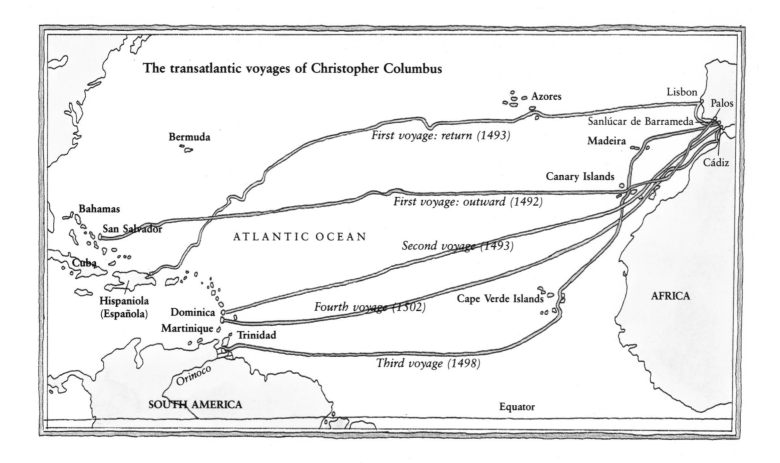

The transatlantic voyages of Christopher Columbus

First voyage: return (1493)

First voyage: outward (1492)

Second voyage (1493)

Fourth voyage (1502)

Third voyage (1498)

Azores   Lisbon   Palos

Bermuda   Sanlúcar de Barrameda   Madeira   Cádiz

Canary Islands

Bahamas

San Salvador

ATLANTIC OCEAN

Cuba

Hispaniola (Española)

Dominica

Cape Verde Islands   AFRICA

Martinique   Trinidad

Orinoco

SOUTH AMERICA   Equator

while Columbus sailed south with the remaining ships, intending to cross the ocean below the equator. But once the ships were past the Cape Verde Islands, the heat was so intense that Columbus headed westward, thereby missing the coast of what is now Brazil, which was later claimed by the Portuguese. He reached Venezuela which he decided was probably part of the huge Chinese Empire.

In August he reached Hispaniola, where he met his younger brother, Diego, in the new town of Santo Domingo. He found the settlers here so rebellious that he appealed to the monarchs for help. A new governor, Francisco de Bobadilla, arrived and arrested Columbus and both his brothers. On October 20, 1500, Columbus arrived in Cádiz in chains.

He was immediately released, but his favor was on the wane. In March 1502, however,

Columbus received authorization for another voyage to sail past the islands he had already explored and find the Indies of his dream. He had once more convinced the sovereigns, but his title Viceroy of the Indies was not restored to him. In the meantime many other navigators, including the Florentine Amerigo Vespucci, had followed him to the New World, landing in both South and North America.

On May 9, 1502, Columbus set off from Cádiz on what was to be his last voyage. Although ships were now sailing regularly between Hispaniola and Spain, he was forbidden to land on that island. Columbus and his four caravels met with many misfortunes. He reached Martinique and warned the fleet in Santo Domingo, which was preparing to set sail for Spain, that a hurricane was imminent. His warning was ignored, and virtually all the

Important Voyages of Discovery After 1492

1497 — John Cabot (Giovanni Caboto) sailed in the service of Henry VII of England and landed in Newfoundland. In 1498, he explored what is now Maine.

1497–1499 — In the service of King Manuel I of Portugal, Vasco da Gama left Lisbon in July 1497. On November 22 of the same year, he passed the southernmost point of Africa, and following the eastern coast, he crossed the Mozambique Channel and was able to reach Malindi (in modern Kenya) on April 14, 1498. From Malindi, when he was assisted by an Arab pilot, he reached Calcutta. He arrived in May 1498 and thus opened the eastern route to the Indies.

1499 — The Spaniard Alonso de Hojeda, once a shipmate of Columbus's, explored the coasts of Guyana in South America. Amerigo Vespucci took part in this expedition, which continued to the mouth of the Amazon River.

1500–1501 — The Portuguese Pedro Alvares Cabral left Lisbon hoping to reach India by circumnavigating Africa; but before rounding the Cape of Good Hope, he crossed the Atlantic and discovered a land that would later be eastern Brazil.

1501–1502 — Amerigo Vespucci, in the service of the king of Portugal, reached the Brazilian coast and probably went as far south as Patagonia.

1506 — The Portuguese Tristão da Cunha discovered the group of islands in the South Atlantic that still bear his name.

1507 — Perhaps in this year the Portuguese Pedro Mascarenhas discovered the islands of Mauritius and Réunion in the Indian Ocean.

1508 — The Spaniard Sebastiano de Ocampo circumnavigated Cuba.

1508–1509 — Sebastian Cabot crossed the Hudson Strait. Juan Díaz de Solís explored the coasts of Honduras and the Yucatán peninsula.

1513 — The Spaniard Vasco Núñez de Balboa crossed the Isthmus of Panama and discovered the Pacific Ocean, which he called "Mar del Sur." The Spaniard Juan Ponce de León explored Florida.

1519–1522 — The Portuguese Ferdinand Magellan, in the service of the king of Spain, left Sanlúcar de Barrameda in September 1519 with five ships. He arrived at the most southerly point of South America in October 1520, and entered the ocean that he would call the Pacific on November 28. With three remaining ships he reached the Mariana Islands and the archipelago of St. Lazarus—the Philippines—in March 1521. It was here, on April 27, that he was killed by natives. One of his ships returned to Portugal via the Cape of Good Hope, and in September 1522 it completed the first voyage around the world. An Italian from Vicenza, Antonio Pigafetta, kept a diary of the voyage.

1524 — The Florentine Giovanni da Verrazzano, in the service of the king of France, crossed the Atlantic to northern Florida and explored the North American coastline up as far as Maine.

1528–1536 — The Spaniard Álvar Núñez Cabeza de Vaca traveled overland from the eastern Gulf of Mexico to California.

1534–1536 — The Frenchman Jacques Cartier reached the Gulf of St. Lawrence, traveled along the river of the same name, and arrived in what is now Quebec.

1540–1541 — The Spaniard Francisco de Orellana traveled the Amazon River from the Andes to its mouth.

---

fleet sank.

Columbus explored the Honduran coast, where he met various native peoples, including the Mayan Cocoms. He sailed along the coasts of Nicaragua and Costa Rica down to the Isthmus of Panama. Here his ships ran aground in an estuary, and Columbus was attacked by hostile natives and by malaria. He managed to set sail again on April 16, 1503, with three caravels, all with damaged hulls. Leaving behind the continent he still believed to be China, he headed for Santo Domingo. At the end of June, he was forced to stop at Jamaica because his two remaining ships were no longer seaworthy (he had abandoned the third two months before). He spent an eventful year on the island, battling disease, intrigues, rebellion among the crew, and the hostility of the islanders. Some of his men managed to reach Hispaniola, and in June 1504 two ships collected Columbus and what was left of his crew. Even the voyage from Santo Domingo to Spain was dramatic, as the damaged ships encountered bad weather. Columbus finally reached Sanlúcar de Barrameda on November 7, 1504. He died in Valladolid, on May 20, 1506, while waiting for an audience with the new rulers of Castile, Joanna the Mad and her husband, Philip the Handsome.

The Orient
India

By a quirk of fate, the Orient, which Columbus had longed in vain to see, became a flourishing Portuguese commercial empire in the years immediately following his death.

When Vasco da Gama first landed in Calcutta in 1498, the political and religious situation of the huge Indian peninsula was extremely complex. For centuries Muslim armies had raided India. The north was ruled by the sultan of Delhi. Although the nature of the relationship between Muslims and Hindus depended on individual sultans, many Hindus remained faithful to their religion, which was based on a caste system. The central part of the peninsula was divided into numerous kingdoms, most at war with each other. In 1526, Babur, a descendant of the Mongol ruler Tamerlane, founded the Moghul Empire, which enjoyed a period of prosperity and cultural riches until its decline in the eighteenth century, when it eventually came under British rule.

China

China at the end of the fifteenth century was very different from the "Cathay" Marco Polo had visited two centuries before. The dynasty of the Khans, Mongol emperors, had been in decline for some time when, in 1368, a nationalist revolt brought the Chinese Ming dynasty to power; it remained in power until 1644. When the Portuguese arrived in about 1514, the ancient Confucian religion was about to supplant Buddhism. Order and discipline prevailed. Culture and the arts, especially painting and ceramics, flourished.

Japan

Japan, where the Portuguese first landed in 1543, was a feudal country in which the emperor had virtually no power, for it was dominated by his general, the shogun, the leader of a small group of feudal lords, the *daimyo*. Samurai, professional warriors who fought for whoever paid them most, came from the lower ranks of the nobility. Life was difficult, especially for the poorer classes, because of continual civil wars. These, however, did not prevent great progress in art and culture.

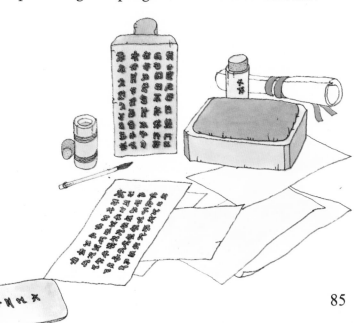

Europe After Columbus

At first there was great interest in the discoveries of Columbus, but they had no immediate effect on the political and economic life of Europe. The stable monarchies of Spain, Portugal, France, and England encouraged exploration but Italy, already ruler of the Mediterranean, was paralyzed by its internal divisions.

Only after the first few decades of the sixteenth century were the full effects of the discovery of America felt (the New World was given the name America in 1507 by a German geographer who had read the diaries of Amerigo Vespucci). Spain paid for its European imports with precious metals from its American territories, and this caused a general increase in prices throughout Europe. Merchants and bankers profited; peasants and laborers suffered, as did the aristocratic landowners.

In spite of the conflicts and differences between individual states, a general philosophical movement known as humanism began toward the end of the fourteenth century and developed during the fifteenth. Humanists emphasized the human being as a free individual, capable of understanding and dominating the world. Humanist thinkers, using Latin as their common language, traveled from one country to another and taught in the great universities.

In Italy and elsewhere humanism affected the arts. During the Renaissance, despite its political instability, Italy was a center for painting, sculpture, and architecture.

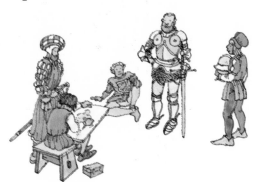

Some Important Dates in European History 1493–1558

1493	The Hapsburg Maximilian I became king of Germany and Holy Roman Emperor.
1494	Charles VIII, king of France, invaded Italy.
1498	Louis XII became king of France.
1502	Peace was established between Venice, the pope, and Hungary on the one hand, and the Turkish Empire on the other. From this time on, Venice was no longer the greatest naval power in the eastern Mediterranean.
1503	Alexander VI, the Borgia pope, died.
1504	Queen Isabella of Castile died. She was succeeded by her daughter Joanna the Mad and son-in-law Philip the Handsome, son of Emperor Maximilian I.
1509	The Dutch humanist Desiderius Erasmus wrote *The Praise of Folly*, against the corruption and ignorance of the clergy. Henry VIII became king of England on the death of his father, Henry VII.
1513	Niccolò Machiavelli wrote *The Prince*.
1515	Louis XII died in France and was succeeded by Francis I.
1516	The English humanist Sir Thomas More wrote *Utopia*. Ferdinand II of Aragon died and was succeeded on the Spanish throne by his nephew, Charles I, son of Joanna the Mad and Philip the Handsome.
1517	The German monk Martin Luther made public his ninety-five theses against the political and religious corruption of the papacy.
1519	Charles I of Spain became Holy Roman Emperor Charles V.
1520	Martin Luther published his treatises.
1527	Rome was sacked by mercenaries of the Holy Roman Emperor, Charles V.
1534	Henry VIII founded the Church of England.
1542	The Council of Trent met for the first time.
1543	Nicolaus Copernicus published his astronomical findings.
1547	On the death of Henry VIII, his daughter Mary, a Catholic, became queen of England.
1556	Emperor Charles V abdicated in favor of his younger brother Ferdinand I, who became Holy Roman Emperor, and of his son Philip II, who became king of Spain and its American dominions.
1558	On the death of Mary I, the Protestant Elizabeth I became queen of England.

Important Dates in Italian Renaissance Art

1419	Filippo Brunelleschi designed the loggia of the Foundling Hospital in Florence.
1420	The architect Luciano Laurana was born.
c. 1430	The painter Antonello da Messina was born.
1431	The painter Andrea Mantegna was born.
c. 1434	Donatello sculpted his bronze *David*.
1438	Fra Angelico painted the frescoes in the Convent of St. Mark in Florence.
1444	Donato Bramante was born.
1446	Brunelleschi died.
1450	Leone Battista Alberti designed the Church of St. Francis in Rimini.
1452	Leonardo da Vinci was born.
1452–1459	Piero della Francesca painted *The Story of the True Cross* in the Church of St. Francis.
1455	Fra Angelico died.
1456–1460	Paolo Uccello painted the three panels of *The Battle of San Romano*.
1465	Piero della Francesca painted the portraits of the duke and duchess of Urbino.
1466	Donatello died.
1468	Laurana worked in the Ducal Palace of Urbino.
1472	Leone Battista Alberti died.
1474	Mantegna finished the frescoes in the bridal chamber of the Ducal Palace in Mantua.
1475	Michelangelo Buonarroti was born. Antonello da Messina painted *Virgin of the Annunciation*. Piero della Francesca painted *The Madonna of Senigallia*.
1478	Sandro Botticelli painted *Spring*. The painter Giorgione was born.
1479	Laurana and Antonello da Messina died.
1483	The painter Raphael was born.
1486	Botticelli painted *The Birth of Venus*.
1487	Leonardo painted a *Madonna of the Rocks*.
c. 1490	The painter Titian was born.

1492	Piero della Francesca died, on October 12, the day on which the New World was discovered.
1495	Leonardo began *The Last Supper* at the Church of Santa Maria delle Grazie in Milan.
1498–1499	Michelangelo sculpted the *Pietà* that is now in St. Peter's Basilica in Rome.
1501	Bramante built the Church of San Pietro in Montorio in Rome.
1501–1504	Michelangelo sculpted the statue of *David*.
1504	Raphael painted *The Marriage of the Virgin*.
c. 1504	Leonardo painted the Mona Lisa.
c. 1505	Giorgione painted *The Tempest*.
1506	Mantegna died. In Rome work began on the construction of the new St. Peter's, designed by Bramante.
1508	The architect Andrea Palladio was born.
1508–1511	Michelangelo frescoed the ceiling of the Sistine Chapel in the Vatican in Rome.
1509–1517	Raphael frescoed a series of rooms in the Vatican.
1510	Botticelli and Giorgione died.
1511	Bramante died.
1518	Titian painted *The Assumption of the Virgin* in Venice. The painter Tintoretto was born.
1519	Leonardo died.
1520	Raphael died.
1528	The painter Paolo Veronese (Paolo Caliari) was born.
1536–1541	Michelangelo painted the fresco *The Last Judgment* on a wall of the Sistine Chapel.
1547	Michelangelo designed the dome of St. Peter's.
1551–1553	Palladio built the Villa Rotonda in Vicenza.
1555	Veronese began the frescoes in the Church of St. Sebastian in Venice.
1560	Giorgio Vasari designed the Uffizi Palace in Florence.
1564	Michelangelo died. Galileo Galilei was born.

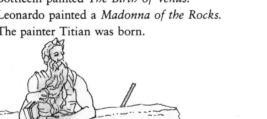

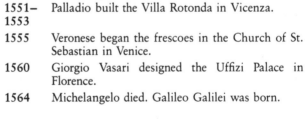

Native North and South Americans

After the European discovery of America, many of the various indigenous peoples met the same fate, although at different times. For the peoples of Central and South America, including modern-day Mexico, the conquest meant the loss of their freedom and often of life, not only as a result of persecution but also because of the diseases the Europeans brought with them. Only a few years after Columbus's arrival the Taino population of the Caribbean was almost extinct. Between 1519 and 1533 the Aztec Empire collapsed. Many Inca were forced by the Spaniards to work in gold and silver mines, where huge numbers of them died.

North American natives survived longer because colonization really began there only in the seventeenth century. However, as pioneers traveled westward and discovered new territories in the nineteenth century, they coveted the rich and abundant territory. As a result, many Native Americans were tricked or forced out of their land.

The Conquest of Mexico

The Spaniard Hernán Cortés left Cuba with orders to explore, and landed in Mexico in 1519 with some six hundred Europeans, two hundred Indians, several Africans, sixteen horses, and fourteen cannons. On the east coast of Mexico he founded the town of Vera Cruz. He became an ally of the Totonacs and Tlaxcaltecs, enemies of the Aztecs, and with a small group of Spaniards moved inland toward the capital of the Aztec Empire. On November 8 he entered Tenochtitlán, where by a ruse he captured Emperor Moctezuma (Montezuma). Cortés disposed of an expedition sent by the governor of Cuba with orders to remove him forcibly from his command. An Aztec revolt forced him to leave the capital, but on June 20, 1520, Moctezuma was killed, probably by his own men, who had accused him of submitting to the foreigners. On August 13, 1521, Cortés laid siege to Tenochtitlán and after three months seized it, only to raze it and build Mexico City on the ruins. Between 1522 and 1524 Cortés conquered Central Mexico.

The Conquest of Peru

In 1526 the Spanish adventurer Francisco Pizarro, who had heard of the fabled wealth of the Inca, explored the coast of what is now Ecuador. He returned to Spain, where he persuaded Charles V to name him captain general and governor of the new territories. In 1531, with three ships, 180 men, and some thirty horses, he sailed from Panama, accompanied by his brothers, Juan and Gonzalo, and his half brother, Hernando. He massacred all the natives on an island off the coast of Colombia where on a previous journey he had been warmly received, and landed on the Peruvian coast and marched inland toward the city of Cajamarca in the Andes. This was the temporary home of the Inca under Atahualpa. In November 1532, Pizarro took advantage of the fear caused by the horses, animals the natives had never seen before; he ordered a massacre and took Atahualpa prisoner. After a farcical trial the sovereign was accused of being a heretic and condemned to be burned to death. To escape this fate, Atahualpa agreed to be converted and baptized, but Pizarro demanded a room full of gold in return for his liberation. The Inca stripped their temples and palaces, and heaped the gold in the capital. In spite of the ransom, Pizarro had Atahualpa strangled in May 1533 and subsequently sacked Cuzco. The natives resisted under the rule of other *inka*s, but after their legendary ruler Tupac Amaru was captured and killed in 1781, the Inca Empire was destroyed forever.

The Horse in the New World

Not until the second half of the seventeenth century, about a century after the first contact between Spaniards and the tribes of the Southwest, did nomadic groups of Apaches manage to capture Spanish horses. The use of the horse spread rapidly eastward among Native Americans, especially in the Great Plains, where there were herds of buffalo. Nomadic tribes who usually spent the summer hunting buffalo on foot, and then returned to the mountains during the winter, were able to stay in the plains all year round, thanks to the introduction of the horse. Tribes with different customs, languages, and origins—Cheyenne, Comanche, Kiowa, Arapaho, and Dakota—developed a similar way of life. They depended on buffalo for survival, and were now able to hunt over vast territories on horseback. Conflict among the tribes grew, and there were frequent battles over territory. For this reason the various tribes of the prairies were unable to form a united front against the European invaders.

Five Hundred Years Later

The tragic fate of the native peoples of North, Central, and South America is given voice by one of their chiefs, Eagle Wing: "My native brothers and sisters and I will leave reminders of ourselves forever in this land. We have given many names and words in our many languages, and countless beautiful things that will always speak of us. Fertile Iowa, the broad Dakotas, and abundant Michigan will whisper our names to the sun that caresses them. The Mississippi will murmur our pain; the thunder of Niagara Falls, the sigh of the Illinois River, the melody of the Delaware—these will echo our song of death. Can anyone listen to this eternal elegy without being moved? Our only sin was this: we had what the white man wanted."

Index